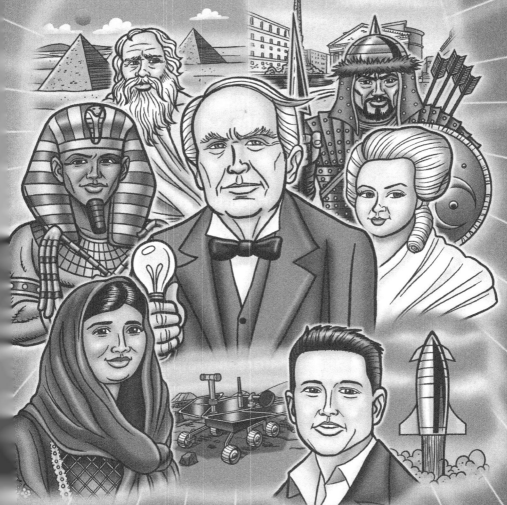

EPIC STORIES FO...

HISTORIC EVENTS THAT CHANGED THE WORLD

RIDDLELAND

TABLE OF CONTENTS

PAGE

Part II: Enlightenment, Colonization, and The Industrial Revolution   52

Did You Enjoy The Book

Other Books By Riddleland

About Riddleland

INTRODUCTION

"What is history but a fable agreed upon?"
- Napoleon Bonaparte

Have you ever been on a camping trip and thrown a piece of paper trash into the fire? Once that paper hits that fire, you cannot bring it back.

History is like that. In world history, there have been at least 55 events that changed the world. These are events that, like the flames of the fire, changed the world so much that the world could never go back to the way it was. Sometimes the flame was an invention; sometimes it was a war; and sometimes it was an idea. In all cases, the world became a different place.

This book looks at those 55 turning points in world history. Each event is recapped, and the person who influenced the event is described. See if you can identify who the famous person is before the narrator reveals the name at the end of the essay.

In addition to an overview of the event and snippets of the life of the person behind it, the person's own words are given, or, in cases where history did not record their words, what others had to say about them. History is more than just dates, names, and places; it teaches us a lot about decision-making and ethics.

Each essay begins with an introduction to show how the event is relevant to one's own life, and, at the end of the essay is a moral that one can learn from the experience.

What has happened in the past has brought us to where we are today, and the decisions we make will determine the world in which future generations will live. The inventions, wars, and ideas have not been limited to one culture – even though our nationalistic pride sometimes causes us to think so, and therefore this book spans the globe. The book begins with the cradle of civilization in Mesopotamia and Egypt in which people used sticks and stones; and concludes with preparations for going to Mars. Along the way it looks at Asian cultures such as the Chinese and Persian; at European cultures such as Greek, Spanish, and English; at African cultures such as Egyptian and South African; at South American cultures such as Incan and Aztec; and at North American cultures, such as Mexican and American.

I encourage you to read the book chapter by chapter. History has a flow, and one event leads to another. To help you see the flow, this book is laid out in chronological order. However, if there are specific events you want to learn about, each chapter is independent of the others, so you can simply skip around if you choose.

Part I

The Rise of Nations

CHAPTER 1

5500 B.C.E.
EGYPTIAN EMPIRE FOUNDED
THE WORLD'S FIRST MAJOR RULER

Have you ever seen a picture of the solar system? The sun is at the center. Mercury is a ball that makes a ring around the sun. Venus is the next ball, and it circles the sun too, but from a distance farther back. After Venus comes Earth, our planet. After Earth, there is Mars, Neptune, and Uranus, respectively. The further from the sun, the less intense the heat is on the planet.

We are like the sun; we see our universe and the people in it revolving around us. Our parents and siblings are the first level; those are near and dear people to us. At the next level

we have our friends. Next, we have our neighborhood, followed by our town. Next, we have our state, our nation, and then all the world itself. That is exactly how civilization has worked too. People began as a small family to hunt berries. By uniting with other relatives, they were able to hunt and trap game. For protection, people started to come together into clans, and then the clans united as nations.

Technology was the secret to raising a nation. Nations could occur once people learned how to farm. Gathering berries and hunting game meant that people had to move as nomads to wherever the berries and game were at that time. Once people learned how to farm, they could stay in one place. Because one person could farm as much as two used to, many in the population became free to become craftsmen and soldiers.

The first civilizations were in Mesopotamia (today's Iran and Iraq). Most significant discoveries came from Mesopotamia, including firsts in clothing, communication, transportation, and shelter. The first major nation, though, was found in the Nile River, not the Euphrates River, where some people had likely wandered.

Egypt became a great nation because it had technology no one else had – the lever. The lever allowed people to move heavy rocks that could not otherwise have been moved. Realizing the great technology before him, Khufu, the Egyptian king around 2700 B.C., commissioned the Great Pyramid of Giza, the oldest and the largest of the Giza pyramids. This pyramid would be a mausoleum for himself as he departed for life after death.

Khufu may have been a very smart person and an extremely ambitious person, but he was also known for being a very cruel, self-centered person. Rather than rule on behalf of the people, he forced his people into coerced labor to construct his pyramid. When it was finished, it was one of the Seven Wonders of the Ancient World.

11

The world was full of petty kings, people who ruled a town or two, and Khufu himself was the son of a king. Khufu, though, was a leader (although one could argue an extremely poor one) who ruled many cities and who harnessed technology. All who saw his pyramids knew he was the most powerful, smartest person in the world.

His father's friends called him Son of Sneferu, and the ancient Greeks knew him as Cheops. The average Egyptian and the history books, though, know this first major ruler as Pharaoh . . . **Khnum Khufu.**

Moral
Technological advances advance society.

CHAPTER 2

3500 B.C.E.
Mesopotamian
Culture Founded

The Stuff Legends are Made of

Have you ever noticed how people like to tell stories about the people they hold in high esteem? For instance, at the Thanksgiving table, I am likely to hear how my great grandpa walked the railroad tracks between my hometown and the next village about ten miles away when he was a teenager just to see a girl. At school, it seems that every year I hear how George Washington chopped down his father's cherry tree and then stated, "I cannot tell a lie." Both stories may have elements of truth in them, but both are so embellished that they are not the exact truth. In both cases, the people who would be able to tell fact from fiction are gone now, so the world will never know exactly what happened.

People tended to tell stories and add in exaggerations about their heroes in ancient times too. For instance, let us consider Gilgamesh, the ancient Sumerian ruler. There likely was a real Gilgamesh, and he likely ruled a group of Sumerians in the city of Uruk in Mesopotamia around 3500 B.C.E. Kings were usually alpha males, so it is highly likely that he was taller than most of his subjects, and, because of his giant size, he was also stronger than most as well. However, to say that he was a partial deity – legend says his father was a priest-king and his mother was the goddess Ninsun and that he had super-human strength - may have been stretching the truth. His deeds, such as bravely killing the monstrous demi-god Humbaba, the guardian of the forest, after everyone advised him not to risk it, were also likely greatly exaggerated.

After Gilgamesh died, people sought to keep his memory alive. Because he was part god, would-be kings liked to show how they were his descendants, justifying their birthright and that they too were gods to be honored. Meanwhile, peasants told his stories orally around campfires and at family gatherings. People would memorize these poems – just like we memorize songs, and they passed these stories on to the next generation. Sumerians invented the alphabet and the concept of writing; they would write on reeds, rocks, and other surfaces. In 2100 B.C.E., these stories were written on tablets. Archeologists have found five separate poems. Around 1600 B.C.E. these poems were compiled into one poem, *The Epic of Gilgamesh*. This was the first major work of literature, and the second major work overall. (The first major work was a religious manual from Egypt.)

The Epic of Gilgamesh, the story of a man on the quest for immortality, likely had a profound effect on both Homer's *Iliad* and the *Odyssey* as well as on the Hebrew *Bible*. The real Gilgamesh never found immortality; sources say he died at the age of 126. The legendary Gilgamesh, though, has recently been rediscovered by archaeologists in 1849, and is having a profound impact on comparative literature and Biblical studies. In that sense, even though he failed in his quest of living forever, he actually succeeded in living forever, for people still speak the name of . . . **Gilgamesh.**

Moral
What you do lives on in other people.

CHAPTER 3

800 B.C.E.
THE ILIAD AND THE ODYSSEY WRITTEN
WRITTEN LITERATURE BECOMES A PART OF CULTURE

The other day I was throwing my frisbee to my friend in the park when he overshot my head. The frisbee sailed into the parking lot, where it came to a halt on some gravel. I was about to get it when I noticed a man was standing beside a van near where the frisbee was. "Don't be afraid, kid," he said, puffing on his cigarette, "I won't hurt you."

His words said he was not going to hurt me, but something about his nonverbal communication told me he might. I stopped walking toward him.

"Come on, kid," he urged. "If you don't come get this frisbee, I may just have to take it home with me."

In the corner of his eye, he could see that my friend had gone to tell our parents at the picnic shelter what was happening. Seeing my friend point at him and everyone looking at him, he picked up the frisbee and threw it to me. I told him thanks and then headed over to the picnic shelter.

I do not know for sure, but I think that man was trying to trick me. Homer knew all about tricks and trickery too. Instead of writing a book like I have done, Homer told stories. Many of Homer's stories were about the Greek siege of the city of Troy which took place in the latter days of the Trojan War. Homer described how some Greek soldiers climbed inside a hollow wooden horse which rested on wheels. Other Greeks then went up to the city walls and quickly retreated, leaving the horse behind. Thinking the horse statue was either a peace offering or

gift soldiers undid the clasp of the horse's belly, allowing the soldiers to get out. One Greek soldier opened the outer gates, and all the other Greeks were able to enter and capture the city with ease.

Little is known about the life of Homer. His two most famous poems, The *Iliad* and The *Odyssey*, were written around 850 B.C.E.; the first tells the end of the Trojan War and the second focuses on the Greek king Odysseus, the king of Ithaca, getting back home from the war. Each work is 24 chapters long; both are poems that were likely written to be sung. The *Iliad* and The *Odyssey* are the two oldest poems in history that have survived intact and been a continuous part of Western society. They were likely sung each year at Greek festivals celebrating the victory over Troy. The stories have stayed relevant, for human nature to trick and deceive is as common today as it was then. Although Homer's works are the oldest in continuous existence, they no longer hold the record for being the oldest literature in existence. In recent times, large fragments of *Gilgamesh* have been unearthed, making it the oldest of all written poems still in circulation.

Whether Homer came up with these ideas himself or if he simply weaved numerous stories into one is uncertain. Homer is typically thought of as being blind in old age, but again nothing can be proven. It has even been speculated that there never was a Homer; doubters believe that Homer is the composite of the achievements of three or four people. About six hundred years later, Plato, the famous Greek philosopher, believed Homer was real, and credited Homer with Greek culture; certainly, Homer was in the first generation of literary Greeks, for the Greek alphabet was not developed until his time. Although not much is known about him, Homer has inspired numerous works of literature and even some works in popular culture. Did you realize that Homer Simpson is named after this man who had no last name but sparked a cultural revolution . . . **Homer.**

Moral
Do not believe everything you hear or read.

CHAPTER 4

700 B.C.E.
GREAT WALL OF CHINA BUILT
THE UNIFICATION OF CHINA

Have you ever sat in a group in which everybody tried to look out for just oneself? Rather than try to see things from other people's perspectives, group members just saw the event from their own perspective. Because everyone wanted it done exactly the way that best suited them, nothing was ever agreed upon or done. Instead of a team, one simply had a group of individuals.

Zheng realized that this is what was happening in China. China was a weak country because lots of small kings ruled different sections of it, and the kings would not work together. Zheng, therefore, conquered each of the small kingdoms. By

247 B.C.E. he united the small provinces into one strong country that put national interests ahead of any petty local interest. Zheng made himself king, starting the Qin dynasty. Zheng did not like the title "king", so he invented a new word, "emperor," to describe himself.

Zheng was worried about outsiders invading China. Beginning in 771 B.C.E., the petty kings had built fortifications and walls to protect their kingdoms from outsiders and each other. Zheng tore the walls that separated the provinces, but he used the technology to construct a 13,000-mile wall containing periodic fortifications. The wall never succeeded at keeping people out, but the wall became a symbol of China's enduring strength and is considered one of the wonders of the world.

Zheng is also known for his huge burial mound and the army of statues of soldiers, the Terracotta Army, that was to guard him in the afterlife, that he had buried with him at the Mausoleum of the First Qin Emperor. Zheng is better known by the name . . . **Qin Shi Huang.**

Moral
"Groups" become "teams" when people work together.

CHAPTER 5

600 B.C.E.
PERSIAN EMPIRE FOUNDED
THE FIRST WORLD EMPEROR

My friends and I like to earn a little spending money, and so we work together mowing people's yards. Before we knock on the person's door to make an offer, we talk among ourselves. We debate what we should offer to do- rake, mow, edge, sweep - and how much we will charge. I may think my friend's price is too high; he may think mine is too low. Once we reach an agreement, then we knock on the door. We may disagree among ourselves privately, but when we are in front of a potential customer, we are both saying the same thing.

Cyrus was a Persian military leader. Prior to Cyrus most of Europe, the Middle East, and western Asia had known kings,

but these were kings of cities or small city-states. These kings were kingly in the sense of being a monarch and having a standing army, but they controlled an exceedingly small area. These were petty kings with small armies, and Cyrus's horde ran over most of them with ease. This empire was not only the first Persian empire; it was the first global empire, having territory in Europe, Africa, and Asia.

Just like my friends and I negotiated details of how we would do the job, Cyrus's generals planned their attacks. Cyrus was not afraid of conflict, and he encouraged his generals to speak up. They did not always agree with one another; however, when it came time to share the final decision with the troops, all the generals were in unison. Cyrus's principle applies not only to the military, but to business and even child-raising.

Being the first person to rule the known world, Cyrus set the standards for future leaders who sought to create empires. Cyrus believed in letting the conquered people keep their own culture rather than thrust them into Persian culture; as long as they respected him and his troops, he was happy. Even though he did not force them to become Persians, many picked up some Persian ways and mannerisms simply by being around the Persians.

Cyrus likely died in battle, but his life is full of myth, so no one knows for sure. Cyrus's tomb is in Iran, and Iranians hold him as one of their heroes. The Greeks called him Cyrus the Elder, for his son continued to expand the empire, most notably capturing Egypt. Other cultures called him Cyrus II for his dad was also Cyrus. The Persians, though, recognized Cyrus was a great man, and it is fitting that in Persia and in the history books, he is known as . . . **Cyrus the Great.**

Moral
It is okay to disagree in private but present a united front in public.

CHAPTER 6

399 B.C.E.
THE DEATH OF SOCRATES

THE SOCRATIC METHOD

Have you ever asked the teacher a question and, rather than answer it, the teacher asked you to first tell her what you thought the answer was? When you answered the question, she likely asked a follow-up question and, once you answered that, perhaps she asked the question of why? Pretty soon, you had answered your own question. This style of teaching is called "Socratic reasoning" and is just one of many remnants of Socrates in our society almost 2,300 years later.

Socrates was a philosopher in Athens in ancient Greece. He did not write down any of his teachings or his methods, but his student Plato provided a detailed biography of him and a collection of his teachings. Scholars are not sure how much of the details in Plato's accounts are the words that Socrates actually said and how much is Plato putting his own teachings in Socrates's mouth. Other sources, such as plays performed in the Greek theater, also mention Socrates, so there is little doubt that he was a real person.

Socrates was likely a former soldier who had turned from the military to be a mason and a philosopher. He was a great teacher, but he ironically referred to himself as a "poor philosopher," so whether he took tuition is questionable. His wife is noted for stating that he did not bring home much money and that he preferred to be around young boys interested in philosophy rather than interact with his own boys.

Socrates may not have been gifted in financial management or parenting, but he was gifted in the art of teaching. One of the principles he taught was to question everything. The government, needless to say, did not appreciate being questioned, and therefore he was charged with "corrupting youth." The city of Athens had a trial, and he was found guilty. His friends offered to help him escape jail; the guard was bribable, but Socrates said that he needed to honor what the city wanted because that was what people in a democracy did. Socrates then drank the poisoned hemlock the jailor gave him.

You may believe that the way we process information, the values we hold, and the way that we reason are natural, but that is not the case; they have been instilled in us by society. All these have roots in Socratic thought. The movement began with Socrates, passed on to Plato, and then passed to Aristotle. Aristotle taught, among others, Alexander the Great, the military genius who conquered most of the known world and spread Greek philosophy everywhere he went. When Alexander shared Greek logic, he was sharing what had been passed down from the teacher who started it all . . . **Socrates.**

Moral
Good questions will lead you to good answers.

CHAPTER 7

331 B.C.E.
GREEK EMPIRE FOUNDED

IT IS ALL GREEK TO ME

Pause for a second and look at a blank sheet of paper.

That paper could be a part of a beautiful picture; it could later contain a great story. It might be the surface that watercolor, crayon, ink, or pencil lead write on. That paper has so much potential. What happens to it depends on who encounters it.

When we are born, we are like blank sheets of paper. Those around us begin to write upon us. Our parents write on us, and so do our teachers, friends, the media, and the government. Each help to shape who we are. We, of course, have the choice of whether to follow their teachings, and, ultimately, we are responsible for what we do.

Alexander followed in his father's footsteps. He was king of Macedonia from 336 – 323 B.C.E. Alexander had the best education a person could have; he was tutored by the philosopher Aristotle who had been tutored by Plato.

Alexander was a military genius. He never lost a battle. (Neither have you nor I for that matter, but, unlike Alexander, we do not battle enemy armies almost every day.) His empire spread from southern Europe into western Asia and northern Africa. He conquered a lot of kingdoms, but he is especially known for conquering the mighty Persian empire and making its territory his own.

Like the Persians, Alexander allowed conquered territories to keep their own culture, however, Greek language and culture greatly impacted the subdued cultures and even echoes into today's culture. Many of our vocabulary words, especially in science, come from Greek terms. The Christian *Bible* was originally written in Greek. Fraternities use Greek letters. Pillars associated with Greek architecture appear on our homes. The days of the week are named after the Romanized names for the Greek Gods, such as Saturn for Saturday. Most children can tell stories about Greek gods and The *Iliad* is required reading in many high school and college classrooms. Many military strategists study Alexander and compare themselves to him.

Alexander contracted a disease in a foreign land and died at the age of thirty-three. Although his official name was Alexander the III of Macedon, most people know him as . . . **Alexander the Great.**

Moral
Appreciate your teachers.

CHAPTER 8

49 B.C.E.

Crossing the Rubicon Founds Roman Empire

There Was No Turning Back

Have you ever had to make a major life-changing decision? A life-changing decision is one that so alters your life that you can never go back to the way things were. A life-changing decision opens some doors in life but closes others. For instance, maybe you had to decide whether to stay with your aunt or your grandma while your parents were out of town for several months, who you stayed with influenced where you went to school, the household rules you followed, and much more. Most people have about six or seven of these major decision spots in their lives.

Gaius had faced that type of life-changing decision as he stood on the banks of the Rubicon. Gaius was a successful Roman general. He and two of his friends had successfully risen to power while their enemies in the Roman senate had decreased in power. Gaius was a good debater, and, because of his recent military victories over Great Britain, he had become

a celebrity as well. His two co-rulers, as well as some senators, were jealous of his success, so they asked him to retire from the military and go to live in Rome.

Gaius stood on the Rubicon banks. If he crossed the waters alone, he would be giving up his political future. If he did not cross, he would be disobeying an order. If he crossed with his army, he would be igniting a civil war. Whatever he decided, there was no turning back.

"The die is cast," he declared, referring to how game players rolled a die or dice and watched as it rolled. With that, he drew his sword and motioned for his soldiers to follow him across the Rubicon.

Gaius was successful in overthrowing the Roman government and installing himself as sole ruler. He was eventually proclaimed dictator-for-life, but, unknown to him, it was not going to be until a natural death occurred. Gaius was popular with the masses, but not with the elite who craved his power. On March 15, 44 B.C.E. Brutus and his brother-in-law Cassius led the Senate in brutally attacking and killing him; this assassination is still recalled in the Ides of March each year.

Gaius succeeded in expanding the Roman Empire and in welcoming foreigners into the empire. As with other leaders such as Cyrus the Great and Alexander the Great, he let cultures retain their native customs if they did not contradict Roman ones. Too, just like Qin Shi Huang, he sought to unite these various kingdoms and cultures under one central government with people acknowledging him as their ruler. He had changed his name when he became emperor, so instead of swearing loyalties to Gaius, they swore loyalty to . . . **Julius Caesar.**

Moral
Look before you leap . . . and, if you decide to leap, then leap with all your conviction.

CHAPTER 9

150

Paper Invented

The First Literate Society

How many times does your teacher say, "Take out a sheet of paper. We are going to have a quiz"? (Every time my teacher says it, I get a knot in my stomach, even when I know the material.)

Isn't it amazing how our teachers just expect us to have paper available? Isn't it amazing how common paper is? Did you realize that before the year 150, there was no paper as we know it? (Can you picture your teacher saying, "Okay, class, take out your papyrus reeds and quill feathers; we are going to have a quiz"?)

Paper had come into existence around 300 B.C.E., but it was nothing like the paper we know – it was made of bamboo. It was expensive and rare, and so important documents were written on animal bones or sheets of bamboo. These documents were heavy, and often required a cart to carry them.

Paper as we know it was likely invented by Cai, a Chinese court official in charge of modernizing the military, in 105. One day, by sewing tree bark, fishnet, and hemp ends, Cai produced a form of paper. He shared his discovery with the emperor, and the emperor encouraged him to proceed. Cai tried various combinations of materials to make the perfect paper. Today's paper is made from milled plant and textile fibers.

The invention of paper for the masses changed the world. Although people wrote on scrolls prior to paper, scrolls were rare. By copying the content of the scrolls on paper, the content became much more readily available. Paper allowed people to have a surface upon which to write and to express themselves. Too, it was light in weight and uniform in height, unlike documents written on bones. The availability of paper led to great works of literature and to a growth of culture.

Literature, the availability of sacred documents, and commentary on the sacred documents, became widespread. When woodblock printing was invented around 200, documents could be mass produced rather than copied merely by hand. Cai's paper was not just used for writing, however. It was also used for packing goods, allowing products to travel great distances and not break. This greatly enhanced commerce and trade.

Not only did China's culture and economy flourish, but the availability of paper changed other traditions as well. Paper became so plentiful and so cheap that around 580, people began to use paper to wipe their behinds after pooping. In 618, it was first sewn into squares and used as tea bags. That is right, writing and reading, transportation of goods, bathroom etiquette, and even tea drinking, have all been influenced by paper, the invention of . . . **Cai Lun.**

Moral
Much that we take for granted was revolutionary when it was invented.

CHAPTER 10

200

Paper Money Invented/ Silk Road Cut

East and West Unite

Have you ever picked up a twig and snapped it? It broke pretty easily, didn't it? Now, pick up two twigs and break them at the same time. It is not as easy, is it? Although I suspect you were able to do it. Next, pick up three twigs and try to snap them. It is getting much harder, isn't it? Let us add a fourth twig. Sooner or later, you are going to get to the point that you will not be able to break the sticks, even though they are only twigs. (If you live in the city and do not have twigs, get your parent's permission, and try the exercise with wooden pencils.)

Instead of using twigs or wooden pencils, Genghis used arrows to make this point. He pointed out that each of his men and their providence was like an arrow. While each man or providence was weak on his own, when they united into one, they became a powerful force. Genghis was a uniter. He united all the tribes of Northern Asia and became their leader; most people believe this was the founding of the country of Mongolia.

Genghis then sought to expand his empire. He and his men were known as ruthless, killing anyone they encountered; that's right, civilians as well as soldiers and women and children as well as men. He created an empire that stretched from northern Asia into China, and, after he was killed in battle, his descendants captured Korea, central Asia, and much of eastern Europe. His empire was literally the size of Africa.

Aside from conquering the world for personal glory, Genghis did not have any big plans. However, his actions brought about particularly important changes. Because he had to supply his army, Genghis established roads throughout the captured territories; this united the captured territories. The areas he conquered were vastly different – central Asia was Buddhist, southwest Asia was Muslim, and Europe was Christian, and he brought them into contact with each other and enhanced interaction among them. If Genghis did not invent the Silk Road, the land and water routes that connected Europe to far Asia, he certainly enhanced it.

Through his conquering Genghis also furthered the concept of money. The Silk Road was a trade route, but muggers often hid along the trails. Paper had originated in China, and so had the concept of paper money. Rather than literally bring the product one wanted to trade, one could simply bring money. (I am guessing you paid for this book with money; if you gave the shopkeeper a goat or something similar, you bartered like people used to do.) Paper money allowed armies and traders to move swiftly since they did not have to carry whatever they wanted to give up for bargaining or carry heavy coins. Genghis never allowed his image to be put on a coin during his lifetime; if he had, we might know the face behind the name . . . **Genghis Khan.**

Moral
Together we can do things no one can do on their own.

CHAPTER 11

206
COMPASS INVENTED
THE CHINESE GOODWILL TOUR

Do you fear change? A lot of people do.

The world around us is changing. I remember when my dad got our first car with a Global Positioning System (GPS) in it. Before then, we had always run directions off the computer or had used the road map. At first my dad did not trust it, but, in time, he got used to it and now uses it any time he has to go somewhere he has not been previously.

Zheng He had seen radical changes in his lifetime. He had been born near modern Laos, but when the Chinese military invaded to claim the land, he had been taken prisoner and made a servant of the prince, Yung Loo. He served willingly, and soon had the favor of the prince. He and Yung Loo became great friends, and often rode into battle together.

After the emperor died, Yung Loo's older brother was to have inherited the throne. However, Yung Loo's brother was dead, so it went to the brother's son, the king's grandson. Yung Loo thought it should have gone to him. Yung Loo, with Zheng He's help, toppled the new government; they installed the prince as Emperor and Zheng He as Chief of Staff.

Yung Loo was an ambitious emperor and set about to conquer Vietnam and Japan. He also wanted to control the Indian Ocean. The Indian Ocean had not been explored, though. Zheng He offered to oversee the building of the new navy fleet - 3,500 ships, and then take a crew and go to explore the Indian Ocean. Yung Loo agreed.

The ships were equipped with the latest technology, particularly the compass. The compass had been invented in China around 100 B.C.E., but it had always been used just for fortune telling and building construction. The compass allowed boats to venture away from the shore, something earlier sailors had not dared to do for fear of not finding their way back. The boats also had the latest in technology for communication, including flags, gongs, carrier pigeons, bells, banners, and lanterns.

Zheng He was given a fleet of 300 ships and 37,000 men to make seven journeys in which he went to over 30 countries in Asia, the Middle East, and Africa. Different ships had different purposes; for instance, one ship carried just horses. The purpose of his journeys was to "wow" people with China's technology, and help these people realize China was the superior country. Trading and treasure were secondary; the Chinese national pride said China had the best of everything so why would it want stuff from other lands. (On the seventh trip, Zheng He did find something no one in China had seen before – a giraffe. He captured a giraffe and zebra to bring back.)

Zheng He explored India long before Vasco Da Gama of Portugal. Although he was a hero in his day, his work was soon forgotten; China changed rulers and the new ruler wanted to spend money on repairing infrastructure rather than exploring and developing foreign relations; he believed China could be self-sufficient and did not need other countries. Zheng He didn't live to see this, however; he had become ill on the return voyage of the seventh journey. His body was likely dumped at sea; no one has ever found it. (If you think it was taken to land and go to China to look for a tombstone, do not look for Zheng He, though; Zheng He was his birth name, but after he became a servant, he changed his name to . . . **Cheng Ho.**)

Moral
Make the most of technology.

CHAPTER 12

476
FALL OF ROMAN EMPIRE
FACTORS LEADING TO THE FALL OF ROME

I moved to South Carolina a couple of years ago. When I went back to Missouri to visit my friends, they all said that I had a Southern accent. I did not realize that I had picked one up, but I had to admit upon carefully listening to myself, I did have a Southern accent.

Rome's armies had conquered a lot of lands, and they too had gradually allowed local elements to creep into their ranks. Whereas the Roman soldiers used to be very self-disciplined, they had lost part of that edge. The fall of Rome did not happen overnight, but it was gradual; It was so gradual that no one saw it at the time.

The blame for the fall does not rest with just the soldiers, however. Leadership also slowly deteriorated. As with most empires, leadership was passed from generation to generation. Some rulers had been good and nurtured the people; others had been self-serving. Some had been competent leaders, and others had little leadership skills. In 476, the last Roman emperor, Romulus Augustus, was merely sixteen.

Another reason Rome fell was that immigrants with no loyalty to Rome were settling on Roman lands. Barbarians, people who could not read and who did not value traditional culture, such as the Germans and the Huns, were rising to power, and people were pouring into the outskirts of the empire to escape the land-grabbing barbarians. Whereas earlier generations on those Roman grounds were patriotic Romans, the illegal immigrants who had the land in 476 had no particular attachment to Rome.

Although no one may have seen the gradual internal collapse, in September of 476 all could see the German general, Odoacer entering Italy, and setting himself up as the new king. (Did you notice that I said king? Odoacer did not want to be called emperor as the Romans had done. A new era was dawning; the Roman Empire was no more.)

For the sake of a smooth transition, Odoacer pretended to be the puppet of the Byzantine empire, that is, the eastern part of the old Roman empire. (This part of the empire would endure for another thousand years until the Ottoman Empire swallowed it.) The greatest example of this servitude was that Odoacer had coins made up with his head on one side and the Byzantine ruler on the other. In reality, though, Odoacer's Italy was completely separate from the Byzantine empire, and Odoacer did not bow down to the Byzantine emperor.

In its glory days, Rome had been the center of science, trade, literature, music, manufacturing, and architecture. The barbarians did not value most of these, and western Europe fell into the Dark Ages. (People did not forget about the Roman Empire, however, and in the Renaissance all of these would become valued again.) The statesman and military genius who put the final nail in the coffin of the Roman Empire and thrust western Europe into a time of chaos full of petty kings rather than one emperor was . . . **Flavius Odoacer (433 – 493).**

Moral
Be mindful of your actions; do not let bad habits creep into your life.

CHAPTER 13

1200

Rise of
Incan Culture

Light, Smoke, and Mirrors

Do you marvel at magic tricks? I know I do. Let me tell you about one that I used to fool my friends with:

I had each person write their name and their weekend plans on a piece of paper. I then held the paper above my head and magically could tell them what it said inside. Everyone was impressed. What they did not know is that a friend had put one in, put an "X" on it, and told me in advance what it would say. I drew out a paper, making sure it was not the "X" and memorized it. I then pretended I had my friend's paper; I told him what he said, and he readily agreed I was right.

People were skeptical, but then I drew out a second piece of paper. I then quoted the name and the contents from the first piece. The person was amazed. I followed this up by pulling out a third piece of paper and repeating what the second paper had said. I kept doing this until the only paper left was the one with

the "x"; I made sure to hide the "X' and I quoted what I had read on the previous sheet.

Manco (1180? – 1230) was likely a magician too. He told people in Peru around 1230 that he was the child of the sun god, and that he had been given a mission to bring them together into an earthly kingdom. When he shared this mission, he looked like he was radiating the sun's light. Lots of people agreed to follow him and his teaching, and he became the founder of the Inca nation. If people had looked closely, however, they would have noticed that he stood on a mountain so that the sun's ball was around his head and that he was wearing silver plaques that reflected the sun.

Most people did not look too hard. They were a superstitious group, and they were honored that the sun god, Inti, had sent his son. They worshipped Manco, and they treated him as a king. Manco relied on the sun god for guidance, and people followed his teaching since they came directly from a deity. Manco was a showman as well as an orator. He claimed the sun god had given his son a walking stick, and, where that stick sunk into the ground was where the city was to be built; the stick sunk in at Kuzco, and that became his capital.

Manco had a sister who he said was the daughter of the sun god. Manco took her for his wife, and they had a son. When Manco passed away, his son became leader of the Inca nation. The Incas, along with the Mayan and the Aztecs, were the primary cultures of South America until the Spanish arrived in the 1500s. Whether Manco actually existed or if future rulers just took that name is uncertain, as are the details about Manco's life. Something certainly happened, though, to turn a bunch of hunter-gatherers into a thriving culture, and so it is highly likely someone did provide the guidance to the people; that someone may or may not have been . . . **Manco Capac.**

Moral
Be skeptical; your eyes can play tricks on you.

CHAPTER 14

1215
MAGNA CARTA WRITTEN

A GOVERNMENT OF CHECKS AND BALANCES

Have you ever read about your high school football team's more recent game in the other school's newspaper? If you have, you probably realized that their reporter saw the same game that our reporter saw, and yet their reporter focused on vastly different aspects.

History works the same way. Historians often say that history is written by the winners, and so what you read is told through the eyes of the side that was successful. The point of view of the other side tends to be forgotten as generations go by. Worse, the winners tend to exaggerate the flaws of the losers.

For example, let us look at King John of England who ruled England from 1199 until 1216. King John was not a wise king, but was he really as evil as he is depicted in the Robin Hood legends? Probably not. However, King John was extremely unpopular with the barons, and they threatened a revolt. King John might have been the king, but, because of his perceived ineptness, they wanted to have control in governing.

Working with the barons and particularly the Archbishop of Canterbury, King John created the Magna Carta; "Magna Carta" is Latin for "Great Charter." The charter allowed the king to retain power, but it created checks and balances so that a naive fool or a dictator could not fulfill their wishes. Likewise, although it gave power to the house of barons, it did not give them full reign over the kingdom. Both the king and the barons had to work together for the good of all.

Although the Archbishop of Canterbury wrote it, when the Pope saw it, he did not approve. Pope Innocent the III opposed the document because it decreased the king's power to order knights to crusades. Although the pope and King John had a rocky relationship – King John had been excommunicated – kicked out – of the church in 1208, he had ultimately bowed down to the pope because he was afraid the pope would ally with France and invade England. (King John was the first, but not the last, English ruler to be kicked out of the Catholic church. King Henry VIII and Queen Elizabeth I would also be excommunicated in later years.) What the pope overlooked or simply took for granted, though, was that the church would remain independent of both the king and the parliament. Stephen knew there was a temptation to make the church and the state one – which is what the pope ideally wanted, but when the state was not following the true God, Stephen realized the church needed the right to protest and therefore they had to be separate.

Neither the king nor the barons were happy with the Magna Carta either, perceiving that the other side had won, and both sides readily violated the agreement. A short war followed. The wisdom of the core concepts of the document, though, was recognized by both the monarchy and the barons. The document was revised in 1216, 1217, and 1225, with controversial clauses being watered down or eliminated. Its principles of checks and balances can be seen world-wide today, including in the English monarchy and in the executive, legislative, and judicial branches of the United States. The Magna Carta stressed that no one, not even the king, was above the law.

The principles of no one being above the law, the government having checks and balances, and the separation of church and state continue to this day, but many have forgotten who first wrote about these. Although the numerous revisions resulted in numerous people contributing to the final draft of the Magna Carta, the first draft of the Magna Carta that laid out the basic principles was written by the Archbishop of Canterbury . . .**Stephen Langton.**

CHAPTER 15

1436
GUTENBERG PRESS
TWENTY-SIX SOLDIERS OF LEAD

Have you ever been assigned sentences to write because you talked in class? I have a teacher who assigns sentences as punishment, and I have had to write, "I will not talk in class" one hundred times. It took me a while, but I did it.

If you have written sentences for a teacher or copied paragraphs from a book for a research project, you know how hard it is. Can you imagine copying a whole book? That is how books were normally copied in Europe prior to the printing press.

Books were rare, and only certain people had access to the books. Because most people could not read Homer or the classics, most people did not know them. Most people did not have access to a *Bible* or to their sacred scriptures either, and they had to rely upon a priest to tell them what it said.

Europeans were aware that the Chinese had invented block printing. With block printing, the words or pictures were carved out of the block, the block was then inked, and then the inked block would be pressed against the page or clothing. Blocks took a long, long time to make, but once they were made, they could be reused many times.

Johanne was a deeply religious German, Christian man who believed that many people were pagans simply because they had not been able to hear the word of God. He believed that if they could just become literate and could have their own copy of the scriptures, they would come to know God. He believed he could create a machine that could print the scriptures and put the scriptures in the hands of everyone. Johanne took lead casting of letters and slid them down iron tracks. He was not the first person to use moveable type, but he was the first to combine it with oil-based ink, adjustable molds, mass-produced moveable type and create the first workable mechanical printing press. He then proceeded to mass produce the *Gutenberg Bible*, the first printed version of the *Bible*.

Johanne's efforts did not go quite as he planned. When people read the *Bible* for themselves, they found things that the church was doing that were not approved in the *Bible*; this would lead to the Reformation. The printing press also led to the Enlightenment, allowing ideas of great Greeks like Plato and Aristotle to interact with contemporary minds. The Reformation and the Enlightenment are not the same thing, but they sprung from the same source – the printing press, and they often crossed paths with each other.

Not only did the printing press bring back old ideas, but it also allowed current thinkers to mass produce their current ideas. News could travel fast, and city-states quickly turned into states and states into nations. The press not only provided news, but also propaganda, feeding the spread of nationalism. Even within existing nations, societies changed. For instance, whereas reading used to be for the upper-class, now materials were readily available for the middle-class as well.

You and I take printed materials for granted, but until 1436, the mass-produced ink-on-a-page type of document that you are looking at right now did not exist. It exists because of the work of . . . **Johannes Gutenberg.**

Moral
The ability to read should not be taken for granted.

CHAPTER 16

October 12, 1492

Christopher Columbus Discovers the New World

The New-Found World

Have you ever been sure of something, but nobody else believed you? The other day, I was sure I was hearing a noise in my bedroom at night. My parents listened for it, but they did not hear it. My sister said I was making it up for attention. My mom thought it was probably a dream. After much pleading, my dad finally got a humane mouse trap and placed it in the room. The next morning – nothing. The next night, I put a dab of peanut butter in the trap to further entice the creature if there was one. The next morning, I found that I had two unannounced guests – a field mouse and a beetle.

Christopher could relate to people not believing him. He believed that the world was round and that he could sail to India by going west instead of east as other boats did.

Lots of people laughed at him; no one wanted to fund him so he could verify his theory. Christopher did not give up.

Christopher stated, "Nothing that results in human progress is achieved with unanimous consent. Those that are enlightened before the others are condemned to pursue that light in spite of the others." Having been turned down in Italy and Portugal, he went to Spain – where he was turned down by King Ferdinand and Queen Isabella. Queen Isabella of Spain, though, was intrigued by Christopher and his ideas, and so she asked him to stay in town and hang around her court. After she had conquered some extremists elsewhere in the kingdom, she diverted money from the military and gave Christopher three ships – the Nina, the Pinta, and the Santa Maria.

Christopher sailed westward from Spain in August 1492 and made land in the Bahamas – not India – on October 12, 1492. Christopher had been right about being able to see West to India, but he had not realized the continents of North and South America were between Spain and India. Queen Isabella had believed that Christopher could save the country a lot of money if the westward route to India was faster; she did not realize it at the time, but her investment would pay off in literal silver and gold, making Spain a world power.

He had accomplished his goal, and Christopher was a hero upon his return to Spain. He made three other voyages to the New World. Although he has since fallen out of favor because of how his discovery impacted the natives, many countries and towns around the world bear his name – Columbia is a country in South America; Columbus, Ohio, and Columbia, Missouri are cities in the United States; and the District of Columbia where the United States capitol is located, bears his name. The United States even has a federal holiday in October, Columbus Day, in his honor. You may wonder how people got "Columbus" from "Christopher." They did not really. His last name was Columbus; he was . . . **Christopher Columbus.**

Moral
Do not give up on a good idea just because someone rejects it.

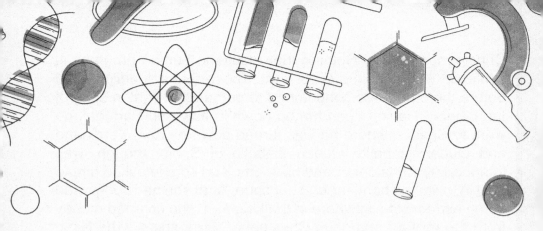

Part II

Enlightenment, Colonization, and The Industrial Revolution

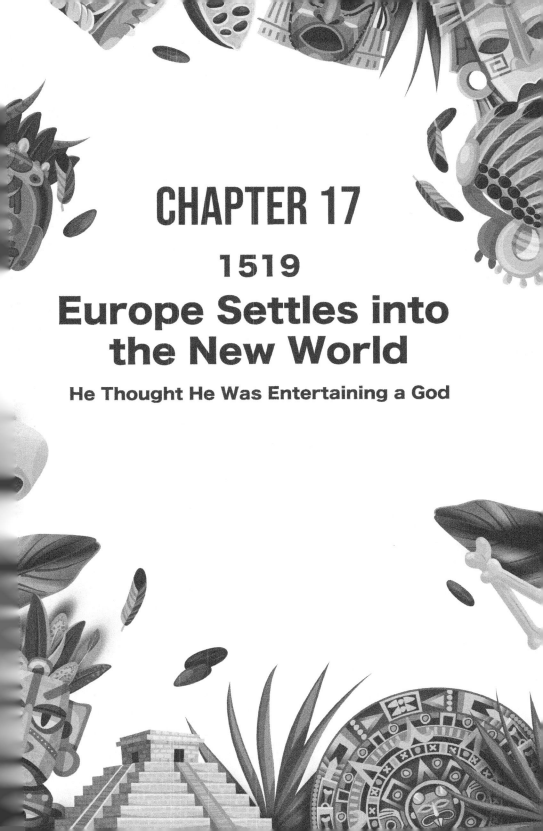

CHAPTER 17

1519

Europe Settles into the New World

He Thought He Was Entertaining a God

Do you remember hearing stories about a family member you had never met, thinking how wonderful it would be to meet this person, and, when you met them later in life, they were not what you expected? At first you may have treated them as if they were a god, but, once you noticed their flaws, you quickly lost some of your respect for them.

If you have, then you can relate to what the Aztec emperor experienced in 1519. All his life, the Aztec Emperor had been hoping to meet Quetzalcoatl, a deity in Aztec mythology whose return was prophesied. The term Quetzalcoatl means "feathered serpent," and that is how the god was sometimes pictured, but it also meant "wisest of men," and this was the form the emperor expected him to take. When the Aztec ruler saw Hernan Cortes, he thought he was meeting with the deity.

Cortes was not a deity, however. He was a Spanish explorer with an army of 400 men he had trained specifically for fighting in the Mexican terrain. He was on the hunt for gold and riches, explaining. "I and my companions suffer from a disease of the heart which can be cured only with gold." The Aztec ruler welcomed him with open arms – and with a gold Aztec calendar which Cortes would later melt for the gold - and took Cortes inside the gate of the capital city, where he dined with what he thought was the deity. The Aztec emperor was honored to have the deity as a guest, and, after the meal, had dancers perform a tribal dance for the deity as a form of reverence as well as entertainment.

Cortes was likely in awe of what was happening. When the Aztec king paid him homage, he accepted it, and he and his men willingly went through the city gate. He had expected a long fight to get inside the city gates, but his men had literally just walked in. Having eaten and seen a few minutes of dancing, Cortes gave the order for his soldiers to draw their swords. The Aztec ruler and his noblemen were captured as prisoners. The Spanish allowed the Aztec ruler to continue to administer daily Aztec affairs as the Spanish prepared for conquest.

Although the Aztec emperor who let the Spanish into the city gates is often branded a superstitious fool, keep in mind that no Aztec had ever seen a European prior to 1517 and that none had direct contact with them until 1519. Prior to his misjudgment of Cortes's character, he was a successful leader. He expanded the Aztec Empire to its greatest height; it stretched from the southern United States through most of Central America. He ruled from 1502 until 1520 with an iron fist and those who dared to challenge his rule faced almost certain death; he was feared, if not respected. Although there were numerous variations of the spelling of this name, throughout the kingdom everyone knew the name . . . **Montezuma II (Sometimes spelled Moctezuma II).**

Moral
Be careful who you trust.

CHAPTER 18

1564

RENAISSANCE AND ENLIGHTENMENT

THE TRUTH MAY HAVE SET HIM FREE – BUT IT PUT HIM UNDER HOUSE ARREST

"Because I said so."

Have you ever heard your mom say that? Mine says it a lot. Whenever she cannot think of a good reason for something she wants me to do, she will simply say that I should do it because she says so. If I try to offer an alternative or prod her to better define her reasoning, she will punish me. "Because I said so" is supposed to be a good enough reason.

Galileo was a scientist who lived in a society that was not interested in all scientific advances. Galileo had constructed a new invention – a telescope – that allowed him to see further into the skies than anyone ever had. Galileo could see the planets Mercury and Venus, as well as Mars and Saturn. As he looked at the planets, he realized that they revolved around the sun, not around the earth.

When Galileo stated his theory to the public, many people challenged it – and him personally. According to church officials, he was daring to contradict the *Bible*. According to the priests, if God said that the earth was the center of the universe, then Galileo's theory must be wrong. (Today's Christians are much more open-minded, realizing that the priest might have misinterpreted the *Bible* or that the *Bible* itself got it wrong. Galileo himself was a Christian his entire life.) Galileo was forced to recant his theory and was placed under house arrest for the rest of his life. In captivity, he wrote books on physics and science, earning him recognition as the father of modern science, the father of the scientific method, and the father of modern physics.

Because he furthered science, Galileo is said to be part of the Enlightenment. This differed from the Renaissance in which the focus was on literature and rediscovering the arts. The Renaissance started before the Enlightenment, but both were going in 1564 when Galileo was born. Because the movements overlap, sometimes they are used as synonyms.

Galileo's inventions and theories pushed the Enlightenment. Although he recanted when his life was threatened, his theory was provable to anyone who was to look at the planets through his telescopes. The telescope would become much more powerful in the days ahead, and society – educators and the church, in particular – had to admit they were wrong and that the person who was right was . . . **Galileo Galilei.**

Moral
Keep an open mind.

CHAPTER 19

MAY 14, 1607
JAMESTOWN, VIRGINIA FOUNDED
SETTLING INTO THE NEW WORLD

I am a collector. (My mom thinks I am a hoarder.) One of the things that I like to collect is travel brochures. Any time that I go to a visitor's center or a hotel, I try to get a brochure of each of the fun things to do in the area. I have my collection sorted by state and then by the type of activity.

Some people can make the most boring place sound interesting. For instance, in South Carolina there is a covered wooden bridge. That wooden bridge was just like hundreds of other wooden bridges in its time. Now, though, that almost all wooden bridges are gone, that bridge is a piece of history, and people will flock from the nearby towns to come see it. A beautiful write up and a couple of catchy pictures in a slick-back brochure makes the bridge a tourist attraction; past generations would have found it mundane and ordinary.

John had the gift of making the mundane sound spectacular. John was a walking legend, having fought in wars, been captured, escaped, and found his way back to England. Exactly how much was true about what he told about himself no one knew; some feared him, and most respected him. He kept his identity a secret on the ship ride to establish the first permanent English colony, Jamestown, in the new world – something that was hard for an egotist like himself to do, but both he and the captain knew that if people found out who he was, mutiny could occur. (The colony was to be named Jamestown in honor of King James; the land upon which it was built was called Virginia in honor of the recently deceased Virgin Queen, Queen Elizabeth I.)

John was supposed to be one of several leaders of the colony, but it was not long before he dominated the leadership council. His rule of "if you don't work, you don't eat" irked the rich, so he was never a popular leader. John did not care about popularity; he cared about keeping everybody alive. Everyone could see that he knew what he was doing, though, and he gladly shared his knowledge, teaching the colonists how to plant. Because the colonists feared the Spanish or the French attacking the fledgling colony of Jamestown to drive the English out of the New World, they welcomed John's military experience and advice as well.

The colonists also feared the Native Americans – and the Native Americans feared them. The Native Americans had mixed feelings about the colonists – they wanted them for allies against warring tribes, but they feared the colonists could turn on them. John dealt directly with the Chief, obtaining much needed corn. One day the Chief sensed that John was being pushy and trying to order him what to do, so he had a brave grab John and place his head upon a rock. He then asked another brave to pick up a stone and bring it down on John's head. The Chief's daughter, Pocahontas, did not want her father to hurt anyone, so she lay down upon John. The Chief then grunted, "Just joking" and said the scene was "an initiation" which John passed.

John explored the new area and drew maps to assist future settlers. He led the colony from September 1608 until August 1609. He was injured when a case of gunpowder went off in his canoe, and he had to return to England. (Or perhaps his powerful enemies got leaders back in England to recall him; it depends on whose version you want to believe.) After he recovered from his injury, John returned to the new world, but not Jamestown, to explore and provide notes about the New England coast.

John wrote glowing accounts about the new world, and his writings helped convince investors to invest in settlements and for people to want to go to claim a piece of land for themselves and start to make their fortune. The American dream of – the opportunity is there if you are willing to work – was born, and it came from the mind of . . . **John Smith.**

Moral
Success requires both deep thought and hard work.

CHAPTER 20

1732
THE FACTORY BECOMES A PART OF LIFE

THE CLOCK BECAME KING

Can you imagine a world without factories?

Before 1732, factories were unheard of. Crafts people worked from their homes at their own pace; they chose if and when they wanted to work. They owned the equipment they used. They set their own hours; there was no time clock to punch. They ate lunch when they wanted, not when a bell told them to eat it. A lunch period could last as long as they wanted; not when the clock struck a certain time. They typically lived in the back of their shop; there was no commute to work. People supervised themselves; there was no boss standing over them. People typically made the product from beginning to end, not just a tiny piece of the product and then pass it on to someone else.

Richard changed all of that. Richard was an inventor, and he wanted to create a machine that would assist in making yarn. He succeeded in creating the yarn machine, but his real accomplishment was unintentional – he changed the structure of society.

Richard was able to harvest river power. Richard realized that flowing water could turn gears that could turn machines. These machines, in turn, meant that people were no longer needed to do certain steps. Richard realized that the remaining steps could be done quickly if each person behaved like a machine - they did a small segment and then passed it on to someone else/fed it into a machine.

Of course, not everyone could afford a waterwheel. This meant the rich who could afford a waterwheel became the factory owners and the poor, those who could not afford a waterwheel, were the workers. As Friedrich Engels and Karl Marx, the men who wrote the *Communist Manifesto*, noted, the rich got richer, and the poor got poorer. In many cases, every family, including children, had to work the grueling shifts in the factories. Engels and Marx urged workers to band together to fight for fair wages. (Some people paid their employees fairly, but others paid them as little as possible.)

Because people had to be at the factory daily – usually for twelve hours at a time for six days a week, cities grew. Some towns were deliberately created by the mill owner, but others simply grew sporadically. Some people lived close enough to where a factory sprung up to commute, but most had to relocate. Because the factory required each person to work a specific piece in the name of speed, it was required for each worker to be present at the same time. Therefore, the clock became king. The person who unintentionally developed the factory system and the modern city was Englishman . . . **Richard Arkwright.**

Moral
The clock can be your best friend or your worst enemy.

CHAPTER 21

1773 – 1788

The American Revolution

"No Taxation Without Representation"

I will share a confession with you – my family came to the United States from Scotland five generations ago and, believe it or not, I do not think very much about Scotland. I realize that the first generation thought about Scotland all the time; they had friends and relatives over there. The second generation may have thought about it some, for they heard stories about how lush and beautiful it was. As each generation became more integrated into American culture, the thoughts of Scotland became less and less.

That is exactly what the colonists in the United States experienced as well. The first generation of settlers was very aware of England and were proud to be English. As generation after generation was born in the thirteen colonies, though, they perceived themselves more and more associated with their colony and less with England.

The colonists realized they had drifted from England and sought a stronger bond with England. For instance, they asked if they could send representatives to the Parliament in London. George, the king of England, told them firmly they could not. Later, when George asked them to pay taxes to offset the costs of the Seven Year's War, Samuel Adams and other colonists chanted, "No taxation without representation."

George believed the war had benefited the colonists and, against his advisors' wisdom, issued taxes on everything from pins to paint – he was intent that the colonists were going to pay. Finally realizing the relations were souring, he removed taxes on everything except tea. George found cheap tea in China and brought it to Boston Harbor; the tea cost so little that with the taxes added in, it was no more than tea used to be.

The colonists were furious over the principle that they were still paying the tax. They asked the Massachusetts governor and petitioned the king himself to remove the ship. Instead, the king parked two more ships full of the tea in the harbor. Seething that the king would not meet their demands of "no taxation without representation," many colonists dressed up as Native Americans, tore open the crates, and dumped the tea into the Atlantic Ocean. This event was known as the Boston Tea Party.

George then passed laws designed to punish Boston and intimidate other cities or colonies from rebelling. In the eyes of all thirteen colonies, these measures were too harsh, and the other colonies came to the aid of Massachusetts. Each colony sent delegates to a Continental Congress in 1775 to orchestrate a response. These delegates were considered rebels in George's eyes. When George sent troops stationed in Boston to find rebel supplies and round up rebel leaders, the colonists concluded that war, not acts of civil disobedience, was the only solution, and at the Second Continental Congress, they did something no colony had ever done – they declared their independence.

In 1778, Benjamin Franklin negotiated an alliance with France, and the French sent soldiers and ships to help the rebels. In 1783, George recognized the colonies' independence at the Treaty of Paris. George wanted to be friends with the colonists, and so he was generous in the settlement, giving them all the land west to the Mississippi. The colonists too, realized their culture was much closer to England's than to France's.

The Congressional representatives agreed how the new nation would be governed - under the Articles of Confederation they had written. These Articles did not work though, so in 1788 the Articles were replaced with the U.S. Constitution. George Washington, the commander of the Continental Army, was selected as the first President.

If King George had just granted the opportunity for the colonies to be represented so they could have a say in how they were governed, the American Revolution might not have happened. However, George was stubborn; some called him "Mad King George." He ruled England from 1760 – 1820; he was the last king over the colonies. Although the loss of the colonies tarnished his reputation, by defeating France in the Seven Years War at the beginning of his reign, conquering India, and then stopping Napoleon, George III is regarded by many in England as a successful king. His birth name was George William Frederick, but he is better known as King . . . **George III.**

Moral
Treat others as you would want to be treated.

CHAPTER 22

1775
THE INDUSTRIAL REVOLUTION BEGINS

GAINING STEAM

Have you ever looked at something and realized that you could make it better? The other day, my dad was lying on the couch. He was hot, and he had turned on a fan. I realized that by turning the fan just slightly, the air would reach him much better. The turn may not have seemed like much, but it made all the difference.

James, too, did something minor that made a big difference. Although James did not invent the steam engine, he added a small twist that greatly improved the existing steam engine. James, a Scottish inventor, realized that the Newcomen steam engine wasted a lot of energy because it had to constantly reheat the cylinder. With his tweaks in 1765, James improved the efficiency, the power, and the cost-effectiveness of the steam engine.

For a steam engine to work, someone had to heat the water in the boiler. This was usually done by burning logs. When the water in the boiler reached its boiling point, the water became steam. When water became steam, it expanded 1,600 times, and that expansion resulted in energy. The pressure had to be released, or else the boiler would explode. (We still use the expression, "I need to let off some steam" when we are upset about something; the expression refers to calming down.) When the pressure was released, it turned mechanical gears that moved the factory machine, train engine, or tractor.

James also came up with the concept of the "watt." A "watt" referred to how strong the engine was. Prior to the steam engine, animals such as horses or oxen, were typically used to make a machine's gears turn. Therefore, an engine was measured in "horse" power; people used the word "horsepower" to describe the power of the engine's strength. A "two-horsepower engine," in other words, could do the work of two horses.

James was an inventor, but not a marketer. Thomas Newcomen had invented the first steam engine, and it was used to pump water out of mines. James realized the steam engine could be used for much more than pumping water, but he was not able to convince many people of this. In 1775, James established Boulton and Watt with Matthew Boulton, and sales began to skyrocket. The sales were so good, James was able to tinker with other inventions the rest of his life and retire as a wealthy man.

Whereas early steam engines generally relied on lumber and other carbon-producing items to heat the water, today's steam engines can be heated by the sun's solar energy. The steam engine is still a big part of society today.

Whereas the factory concept was developed by Richard Arkwright, the machinery for the Industrial Revolution relied upon James's steam invention. If the Industrial Revolution is to be credited to any one person, that person would have to be . . . **James Watt.**

Moral
Pressure is good, but too much pressure is bad.

CHAPTER 23

1789-1799
FRENCH REVOLUTION
DEMOCRACY – LIKE IT OR ELSE!

Have you ever been around people that you knew were not cheering for the same side that you were? The other day my family and I went to a Super Bowl Party. I wore my Kansas City Chiefs jersey with pride. Imagine my shock when I saw other people sporting Tampa Bay Buccaneers caps and jerseys. It did not take me long to realize that although we were all part of the same group watching the same television, we were not all cheering for the same outcome.

Max was a French lawyer. He had made a lot of money in the early part of his career, and he had turned his attention to defending the poor who could not afford a lawyer. He was known as "Mr. Incorruptible" because of his strict moral values.

Max argued against class privilege, and he became extremely popular with the people. He was elected president of the Jacobin political group, and he and his followers revolted against the king, wanting a government of the people and by the people. They arrested the king, King Louis the Sixteenth of France, and had him beheaded in December 1792, declaring, "The king must die so the country can live."

Max believed that France needed a democracy. He was one of the authors of the *Declaration of the Rights of Man and Citizen*, which became the foundation for the French constitution. Max believed, "Any law which violates the inalienable rights of man is essentially unjust and tyrannical; it is not a law at all."

Did I mention that Max believed France needed a democracy? Ironically, he believed it so much that he executed anyone who opposed him. He declared, "Terror is only justice: prompt, severe and inflexible; it is then an emanation of virtue; it is less a distinct principle than a natural consequence of the general principle of democracy, applied to the most pressing wants of the country." During this Reign of Terror 300,000 people were arrested and over 17,000 people were executed.

Believing that Max had gotten drunk off power, members of his own political party had him arrested on July 27, 1794. A sympathetic jailor, though, let him go free. Max escaped to City Hall, where he attempted suicide. His suicide attempt failed, and he was arrested; he was beheaded the next day.

Without Max's iron hand forcing democracy and a political ideal, corruption entered the party. Party officials began to behave like the royalty they had so despised. With the ideals gone and corruption rampant, people lost respect for the revolution. In 1799, Napoleon Bonaparte overthrew the party members and, in 1804, declared himself emperor.

Most people in history are painted as either heroes or villains, and few people look close enough to see that all people are both. Max, though, was a hero and a villain at the same time, championing the rights of the people while also overseeing a Reign of Terror. History may not know how to classify him, but it certainly knows the name of . . . **Maximilien Robespierre.**

Moral
Do not let power corrupt you.

CHAPTER 24

1791
OLYMPE DE GOUGES

IT'S MORE THAN ENTERTAINMENT . . . BUT DON'T TELL THE MEN

In Europe in the 1700s the great philosophers looked around them and formulated natural law, a philosophy that studied nature, and then concluded that there were natural orders. One of the things they noticed in human society was that males were dominant over females, just like animals were in the wild, and they proposed that this was how society should be set up.

That notion was relatively unchallenged until 1791, when a female French playwright, Maria, published the *Declaration* of the Rights of Woman and the Female Citizen; in this work she stated, "All citizens including women are equally admissible to all public dignities, offices and employments, according to their capacity, and with no other distinction than that of their virtues and talents." Needless to say, the men in power were not pleased to hear that women wanted a share of the power, and she was one of numerous people guillotined during the French Revolution.

Just as people today who would not listen to a radical preacher speak would listen to a television character talk under the guise of "entertainment," her plays put unheard of ideas in front of the international community. These ideas became the seeds of the women's suffrage movement. Although her plays were very popular in her time and she was a well-known celebrity, she was forgotten by history, but her accomplishments were not. As scholarship into women's rights has increased in the past decades, she has been rediscovered. Although later overshadowed by others in Europe and North America, the seeds of the Women's Movement that changed the world were planted by Marie Gouze who went by the pen name . . . . **Olympe de Gouges.**

Moral
All people – regardless of gender, race, or religious beliefs – are equal.

CHAPTER 25

1796

Vaccinations are Created

The Doctor Who Deliberately Made His Patients Sick

Do you go to the doctor when you are sick? Most people do. The doctor has advice and medicine for getting well.

Do you go to the doctor when you are well? Believe it or not, most people do, and I suspect you have too. The doctor sometimes gives us shots that help to keep us well. Have you ever wondered what is in those shots? Believe it or not, it is something harmful to you. That is right, the doctor is giving you something that – if given in large doses – could kill you.

The doctor gives you a small dose of the bad bacteria so that you can build up an immunity to it. That is right, having been exposed to the bad bacteria, your body is now ready to fight the bacteria should you come across it again. These shots with the deadly bacteria given in small doses are called "vaccines."

Ed, an English doctor, came up with the idea for vaccines around 1796. At that time, a lot of people were getting smallpox, a very deadly disease. Ed noticed, though, that not all groups of people were getting hit as hard by it. In particular, he noticed that the milkmaids, the women who milked the cows, were not getting it nearly as much as anybody else. He wondered what they were doing differently.

He watched the milkmaids carefully to see what they did differently in their lives than anybody else was doing. He realized that the answer had to lay in the milking. Upon closer examination of the milking process, he noticed that the milkmaids were being exposed to cowpox. Their bodies, though, fought off the cowpox, and that in turn enabled them to fight off the smallpox.

Ed had an idea that sounded like that of a mad scientist: What if he exposed healthy people to cowpox and made them a little sick? Deliberately making your patient sick was not something doctors had ever done. He reasoned that having been exposed to cowpox, his patients would have antibodies to fight off the smallpox. Such an undertaking had never been done before. Ed decided to try it. He gave people shots of cowpox; "cowpox" translates into Latin as "vaccine," and in time "vaccine" became the word used to describe any harmful bacteria being placed in one's body. Ed's idea worked. As more and more people got the shots, the disease was unable to spread and eventually virtually died out.

Today, we have vaccinations for Covid-19, smallpox, and lots of other diseases. By getting exposed to the disease in a small dose, we can handle being exposed to it later in a larger dose. Most of us have immunizations as infants and then periodically after that. (Some people, called anti-vaxxers, do not want to put the deadly viruses into their bodies at all.) To go to school and many public places, vaccines are required. People are living a lot longer nowadays, thanks to "the father of immunology" . . . **Edward Jenner.**

Moral
Stay up to date on your immunizations.

77

CHAPTER 26

JUNE 18, 1815
WATERLOO
HE OVERLOOKED ONE THING

Do you know what you are going to be doing in fifteen years? Can you see what profession you are working in? Can you see what your exact job is? Can you tell if you are working in a small town or city? The clearer you can see the future, the more likely you are to bring about that future.

The goal "to get a job" is very vague, but to say, "to become a veterinary assistant for an animal hospital in a rural community" is extremely specific, and you can begin to study science to prepare for the job. The clearer your goal, the more likely you are to make it come to pass.

Napoleon had goals — first to be a good soldier and, later, a good emperor. Napoleon was a soldier during the chaotic times of the French Revolution. When other kingdoms saw that the French had executed their king, the rulers of some of these other kingdoms attacked France, hoping to put down the revolution so that people in their own countries would not get the idea of deposing them. Napoleon was one of the soldiers who defended the empire, and he quickly rose through the military ranks to be its leader.

When he noticed that the empire was decaying from the rebel leadership, he conducted a coup, taking over the government in 1799. Coalitions of other nations continued to come against France, but he won most battles and even took over their territories. Soon, he had a large empire.

Napoleon shared the French Revolution ideas with all these conquered countries, including Switzerland, Germany, and Italy. He changed the thinking of Europe, promoting secular education, religious toleration, property rights, and equality before the law.

Napoleon had defeated Russia in 1807 and decided to follow-up with an invasion in 1812. The French invaded in the summer but were not prepared for the Russian winter. Napoleon had to retreat and lost much of his army. Seeing Napoleon retreating, the Austrians and Prussia joined Russia, and, in 1814, they marched into Paris, restored the king's family to the throne, and placed Napoleon in exile on the island of Elba.

In February 1815, Napoleon escaped from Elba by boat and returned to France. Upon seeing one of the French king's soldiers guarding the coast, Napoleon raised his hands and said, "Here I am. Kill your emperor if you wish." The soldier, who was supposed to be loyal to the new king, rushed over to Napoleon and gave him a hug. As the soldier headed back to Paris with Napoleon, more and more people followed them. When they got to Paris, Napoleon staged a second coup.

The Prussians and the British were coming to the aid of the French king, so with an Army of 200,000 men, Napoleon went up to Belgium to cut them off. The battle of Waterloo did not go Napoleon's way, and he had to retreat. Knowing his enemies were going to successfully invade Paris and knowing the Prussians had a dead-or-alive warrant on him, he left his son in charge of the government in Paris and fled town. All the ports were blockaded by the British, and he could not flee the country. Seeing he was trapped, he surrendered to the British and was exiled a second time.

Napoleon had a vision, and he almost made it come to pass. He had forgotten how harsh Russian winters were, though. That little detail completely derailed his dreams. When we plan, we must try to think of everything. Business leaders and military strategists, you and I, can learn a lot from one of the greatest organizational minds the world has ever seen . . . **Napoleon Bonaparte.**

Moral
Dream in detail.

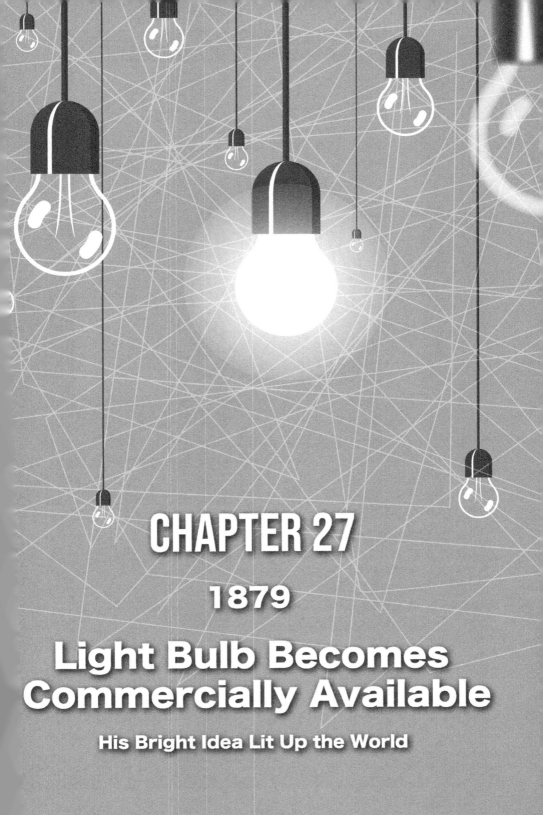

CHAPTER 27

1879

Light Bulb Becomes
Commercially Available

His Bright Idea Lit Up the World

Sometimes I feel like just giving up. I try something, and I try it, and I try it, and each time it ends in failure. For instance, the other day I was playing a video game and I was supposed to leap from one side of the screen to the other. I tried, and I tried, and I tried. I failed every time. I knew, though, that it could be done. I knew that other people had tried and failed, but many of them had kept trying until they got it right. With a try, try, and try again attitude, much can be accomplished.

Thomas is considered one of the best – if not the best – American inventors. Thomas would be the first to tell you that he often did not experience success, but he would never admit failure. He stated, "I have not failed. I've just found 10,000 ways that won't work." Thomas kept trying until he got it right.

Thomas did NOT invent the light bulb. An Englishman named Humphry Davy invented it in 1809. Humphry took two wires and a battery and hooked the wires to a charcoal strip that glowed when the electricity was passed through it. Another inventor, Joseph Swan, installed electric lights in his home in 1867, a decade before Thomas came out with his light bulb. In 1877, though, Thomas improved the light bulb. Thomas believed, "There is a better way for everything. Find it." His improved light bulb became a commercial success.

Prior to the light bulb being available to the public, public streets were lit at night with kerosene lights. Homes had fireplaces and oil lamps. Both factories and farmers had to structure their day around the sun; when there was no sun for light; there was no way that much work could be done. With the invention of a commercially available light bulb, all of that changed – for better or for worse depending on one's perspective. Public streets were now brighter and safer, for most criminals did not want to be seen, but the electric lights lit the city so bright that many star gazers could not enjoy constellations in the sky. The commercial light bulb meant that homes no longer had to have the heat of a fire for light, nor did they needed to maintain open candle flames which often resulted in house fires. The light bulb meant that factories were no longer restricted to day lighting; they could operate 24-hours per day.

The light bulb changed the world. However, it was not just the light bulb – the light bulb had been invented 68 years earlier, it was the improved light bulb Thomas made and the marketing that he gave it. The light bulb was not the only thing Thomas invented; Thomas had 1,093 U.S. patents. In particular, he is credited with inventing – or at least significantly improving -- the motion picture camera and the phonograph. The world would be a much darker place if it were not for . . . **Thomas Edison.**

Moral
Do not give up.

CHAPTER 28

1908
MELITTA BENTZ
COFFEE, ANYBODY?

Do you like coffee? I personally do not, but a lot of my friends do.

Many adults, it seems, have coffee every day as part of their early morning ritual. In many houses, waking up to a pot of coffee brewing is a daily tradition. Pots of coffee are found in almost all restaurants and offices. (Pardon the pun, but office work has its perks.)

People might not be so gung-ho on coffee, though, if it wasn't for the invention of the coffee filter. The invention of the coffee filter didn't happen overnight. It began one morning in 1908 when a German housewife was engaged in the daily task of pretending to like coffee. She drank it because those around her pretended to like it; she didn't realize that they too were just pretending.

Coffee prior to 1908 was made by taking coffee grounds that were in a silk bag and then steeping them in boiling water. The result was a bitter, gritty drink; many of the grounds escaped in the steeping process. (If you have ever had a coffee filter slip and grounds get through, you can experience this gritty drink of yester-year first-hand.)

Believing there had to be some way to remove the grit, the housewife experimented. After she realized there was no effective way to fish the grounds out of the brewed coffee, she wondered if there was a way to prevent them from getting into the water in the first place. Believing that there was, she took a sheet of absorbent paper from her son's school supplies, used a nail to puncture small holes in it — smaller than the coffee grinds — placed the paper above a brass pot, and poured boiling water over it.

She tasted the resulting beverage and loved it. She then shared cups of it with her friends, and they too liked it much better than the traditional coffee. Convinced she was onto something, the 35-year-old began to sell her invention from her home. Before long, she had a factory with four employees.

Her business then grew exponentially. She didn't stop inventing, though. In 1936, she came out with cone-shaped paper to complement her flat paper. Coffee has impacted cultures throughout the world. People take coffee and the coffee filter for granted, but every sip should remind you of . . . **Melitta Bentz.**

Moral
If you see a problem but don't solve it the first time, keep trying.

CHAPTER 29

JUNE 28, 1914
ASSASSINATION OF DUKE FERDINAND II/WORLD WAR I BEGIN

THE CAR RIDE THAT CHANGED THE WORLD

Do you like riding in cars? I do.

Most car rides go very smoothly; we arrive at our destination without an incident. Other trips, though, have not been that smooth. One day my dad and I were driving down a city street when we had to stop for a red traffic light. A distracted driver then ran into the back of us. Luckily, I had my seatbelt on. The man told my dad, "I am so sorry and so embarrassed. Just last week my son did the same thing, and I fussed for days at him." Another time, we had a tire blow out as we turned on a city street. Also, there was a time when the engine light came on and smoke started to pour from under the hood.

My car rides are not nearly as exciting as the car rides of Archduke Franz Ferdinand II of Austria on June 28, 1914. On that day, he and his wife Sophie took a train to Sarajevo, the capital of the Austro-Hungarian province of Bosnia and Herzegovina. At the station, they then got in the third car of a six-car motorcade. Unknown to them, Gavrilo and six other assassins lined the route in seven different spots. The first assassin lost his nerve as the archduke's car passed, but the second threw a bomb under the archduke's car. The grenade had a ten-second delay, so the archduke's driver sped up; the archduke was unhurt, but the bomb injured the people in the next car. Because the convoy traveled fast the rest of the way, Gavrilo and the other assassins were not able to make a second attempt.

When the archduke, the future ruler of Austria, got to the town hall, he angrily declared, "So this is how you welcome your guests – with bombs!" Most of the people in the providence, though, did not want to be a part of Austria-Hungary; they sought independence from Austria, and many may have secretly wished the assassination had succeeded. The archduke made his speech without incident. On his way out of town, he asked the motorcade to make a stop at the hospital where those injured from the grenade were staying so he could personally check on them. His general planned a route that would keep the archduke's car out of the city center and dead-end streets where it could be trapped. The general forgot to tell the duke's driver the final version of the plans, however, and the archduke's car turned down a side street. Realizing the side street was a bad idea, the driver tried to turn around, but the gears locked and the engine stalled. Gavrilo had been standing discreetly by a local delicatessen; he and his friends had again tried to guess the archduke's route to assassinate him. Gavrilo stepped to the car, drew his gun, and fired at point-blank range, hitting the archduke in the neck and his wife in the abdomen. Both died within minutes.

All seven members of the assassination squad were arrested. Gavrilo was only 19; that was too young for the death penalty. He was tried and found guilty. At the trial, he stated he had killed the archduke so that his country could be free; he apologized for killing the duchess, saying it was not intentional. He viewed himself as a patriot and had no remorse for killing the archduke. He admitted being associated with the Black Hand, a revolutionary group sponsored by Serbia. He was then placed in jail, where he died in prison of tuberculosis. In Serbia, people declared him to be a hero, but in Austria he was a villain.

A month later, Austria would declare war on Serbia. The Russians came to the defense of Serbia. Austria and Germany had an agreement that if either were attacked, the other would come to help it defend itself, so when Russia attacked Austria, Germany then came to help the Austrians. Because of alliances, the whole world was soon engaged in the War to End All Wars, the Great War, or, as it came to be known later in history, World War I. The assassination of Archduke Franz Ferdinand II of Austria was the spark that lit World War I; the man who created that spark and changed the world was . . . **Gavrilo Princip.**

Moral
The smallest action can have major consequences.

When you sit in the classroom, who holds the power? If your class is like mine, it is the teacher. How did the teacher get that power? I pondered this, and came up with five ways:

1) The teacher has been appointed by the principal; the administration says the teacher has the power.

2) The teacher can reward students; she has gold stars, and she can give special privileges such as going to the front of the line.

3) The teacher can punish students; she can take away our recess time or talk to our parents.

4) The teacher has our respect; she has our admiration, and we want to please her.

5) The teacher knows more than anybody else; she has a college degree and is the smartest person in the room.

To be in power, a person needs at least one of these sources. The more of these five traits a person has, the more secure in power they are.

Russia was in an alliance with Serbia, and so Russia had been drawn into World War I. The war, though, did not go well, and Nicholas II, the czar — a fancy term for "king" - of Russia was in trouble. His military had been defeated in many battles with the Germans, and people had lost respect for him. Workers had banded together and were expressing their displeasure by going on strike, and this further alienated the czar's followers. To keep the country together, the czar stepped down, leaving his administration to govern with community assemblies known as "Soviets." The new government, though, was no more popular with the average Russian citizen, for it continued to engage in World War I.

Many Russian soldiers mutinied and, together with the workers, they formed an army, the Bolsheviks. ("Bolsheviks" is Russian for "one of the majority.") Vladimir Lenin was their leader. They pledged if they took power, they would end the war. In October 1917, they attacked and overthrew the provisional government, giving all the power to themselves and the assemblies (Soviets). Following the example of the French Revolution, they established a secret police force that would remove, punish, or even execute anyone who dared to defy them.

They ended the war with the Germans as promised, but chaos remained in Russia as other social factions fought the Bolsheviks for power. The Bolsheviks held onto power and changed their name to the Communist Party. They set up Soviet style governments in the newly independent countries of Armenia, Azerbaijan, Belarus, Georgia, and Ukraine. In 1922, the Bolsheviks merged these countries with Russia, calling the new country the Union of Soviet Socialist Republics, better known by the initials U.S.S.R.

Karl, a German who had moved to London, had written the *Communist Manifesto* with Friedrich Engels in 1848. In it, he had described a utopia where each person gave their best work and all people had their needs met - "From each according to his abilities, to each according to his needs." The Soviets tried to put this into practice, giving the farmlands of the rich to the peasants. Karl believed the rich would never give up their lands voluntarily, and he had predicted that communism would have to use force to establish itself, and he was right. Believers of communism hoped this was just the beginning, and they waited for the movement to spread, the social change foreseen and inspired by . . . **Karl Marx.**

Moral
Having a fancy title is not enough to keep you in power.

CHAPTER 31

JUNE 28, 1919
TREATY OF VERSAILLES ENDS WORLD WAR I
SEEDS FOR WAR

    Have you ever planted a seed in a Mason jar, watched it put down roots, and then break its green nose through the soil? The plant will then put down deeper roots and grow taller, its leaves bending to wherever the sun is. Eventually, the plant will outgrow the jar and will need to be transplanted into either a field or a flower bed.

I planted a seed of corn once and had to transplant it shortly. (My mom was not too happy about a corn plant in her flower bed, but she did turn over a small section of it to me.) By the end of the growing season, the plant that began as the size of my fingernail was taller than I was. It even bore several ears of corn. I found it amazing what happened from that one little seed.

Little seeds often put down roots and then become big plants. At the end of World War One, the seeds were planted for Adolf Hitler to rise to power in Germany and bring about World War II. It took about 15 years for the Nazi plant to put down roots and grow, but the roots started the day World War I was declared over.

World War One ended at 11 a.m. on the 11th day of the eleventh month of 1918; i.e., November 11, 1918. That day is still a federal holiday in the United States; we call it Veteran's Day.

On November 11, 1918, all the countries that signed the armistice agreed to stop fighting. The war ended in an armistice, not a surrender. A few months earlier, it appeared Germany would win the war, but then the United States had entered the fray on the side of the Allies, and now it was clear that Germany would likely lose. Since the Allies had the upper hand, they declared that Germany had started the war and that Germany should repay them for the damages it had caused. The Allies also seized territory from Germany and reduced the German military's size with the goal of keeping it weak. The German negotiators felt they had no choice but to agree to these harsh conditions.

A young German soldier named Adolf was one of the majority of Germans who saw the treaty as unfair. Adolf had grown up in Austria-Hungary, but at age 13 had moved to Germany. He served in the German army during World War I and became a decorated soldier. He joined the German Workers' Party in 1919, a far-right group that considered the agreements that ended World War I to be invalid because they were written by German traitors, and, when the Workers' Party became the Nazi Party, he was named leader in 1921. As leader, Adolf made a lot of anti-communist, anti-capitalism, and anti-Jewish statements and went on record saying he greatly opposed the Versailles Treaty. He tried a coup in 1923; it failed, and he was sentenced to five years in jail. While in jail, he wrote the autobiographical book *Mein Kampf.* (That is German for My Struggles.) He got an early release in 1924.

In 1932, the Nazi Party won the most — but not a majority of the seats — in the national election. They persuaded the current president to appoint Adolf as leader. Once installed as leader of Germany, Adolf changed the government into a Nazi dictatorship. Under his guidance, Germany pulled out of the Great Depression; he was also able to annex heavily German-populated lands which Germany had surrendered at the end of World War I. All this re-instilled German pride, as did his daring to defy the agreement not to rearm, and Adolf's popularity in Germany increased each day.

For six years, France, the United Kingdom, and the United States watched as Adolf became more and more aggressive. They did not want war, and so they let him get by with it. They made it clear, though, that if he became too aggressive, they would have to step in. On September 1, 1939, Adolf invaded Poland. France and the United Kingdom felt they had no choice at that point but to declare war on Nazi Germany and on its leader . . . **Adolf Hitler.**

Moral
Be fair when negotiating and the result will likely stand; if you make it greatly in your favor, the other side is not likely to abide by it.

Part III

Globalism

CHAPTER 32

MAY 27 – 28, 1927
FIRST TRANS-ATLANTIC FLIGHT
FROM NEW YORK TO PARIS NONSTOP– IN JUST 33 ½ HOURS

Everything that we do – or do not do – has a risk associated with it. Did you realize that something as simple as getting out of bed in the morning has a risk; you might slip and fall when you put your foot down. Meanwhile, any time you take a test, you risk failing. Of course, if you do not take any tests, you avoid failing but you never pass a test. To be successful in life we must take risks – we need to get out of bed, and we need to take tests.

Although we cannot get rid of all risks, we can greatly lower the risks. For instance, to enhance our chances of not falling, we do not mop our tile floor with cooking oil. Likewise, to enhance the chances of passing the test, we study. Although we cannot get rid of all risk, we can get rid of most of it.

Charles knew how to reduce risk. Charles was an air mail pilot. He loved to fly, and he was good at it. In 1919, a hotel operator offered $25,000 – that would be like someone offering $367,901 today -to anyone who could fly from New York to Paris or from Paris to New York. Eight years had passed, and no one had successfully done it. Charles verified the offer was still out there, and then he set about preparing for the flight.

Charles was NOT the first person to cross the Atlantic. North America and Europe are remarkably close together at Newfoundland and Ireland, and two British pilots had made that trip in 1919. Charles was going to make the first SOLO trip and he was going to do it from a much, much, longer distance - New York to Paris – and he was going to do it nonstop!

In the early morning of May 27, 1927, Charles took off from Roosevelt Field, Long Island, New York. Charles had prepared well, and he was confident that he was likely to land in Paris, but there was no guarantee. As he flew the 33 ½ hours to Paris, he knew his odds were decreasing at certain points – such as when he had to go through several hours of a blinding fog and when he went through a couple of hours of storm clouds – but he kept on flying. Charles did not have a radio with him; the radio would have added extra weight and it was not reliable. You might have thought that once he was over the ocean and back on land that his life would get easy, but it did not. People had come out to see him land and their rows of car headlights made it hard to find the landing lights. At 10:22 p.m. on May 28, Charles landed in Paris and received a hero's welcome.

Charles became the first international superstar; he went from an unknown mail carrier to a celebrity almost overnight. His actions created a great interest in flying, and the world became knit together tighter and tighter. Charles had done what no one else had, but in a few years what he had done would be common-place, and the risk would be less and less. People recognized the risks he had taken, and he earned the nickname "Lucky Lindy." A year later, he would donate The Spirit of St. Louis to the Smithsonian Museum, where it still is today. You can see it and think about the man who spent 33 1/2 memorable hours in it over the Atlantic. . . **Charles Lindbergh.**

Moral
Everything involves some risks.

CHAPTER 33

September 1, 1939

World War II Begins

How Much Change is Too Much?

Do you have a pet? My family is a pet family. We have had goldfish, a hermit crab and a dog. I like to take pictures of my pets. The trouble is my pets do not always want their picture taken. For instance, I may see the most beautiful pose by my dog, but by the time I get my camera ready, my dog has moved. The new picture opportunity may be even more beautiful than before – or it may be worse, but it will certainly be different. If I do not like the pose I see at that time, I can wait for it to change – I can even try to create the change.

Adolf Hitler, the German leader, was a change maker. He did not like the world as he found it, and he wanted to change it. In his opinion, the Versailles treaty that ended World War I was very unfair to Germany, and he wanted to return Germany to a top tier nation.

Neville, the English Prime Minister, understood where Adolf was coming from. He too felt the Versailles treaty was harsh on the Germans, and so he was willing to let Hitler reclaim part of Czechoslovakia in 1938; it was mostly Germans who lived there, and they wanted to be a part of Germany anyway. He went to Munich, Germany, with his French and Italian counterparts, and signed an agreement letting Hitler have the land he wanted.

Neville had lived through World War I, and he and almost everyone else in the United Kingdom had seen enough war; they wanted to avoid war, even if it meant looking weak. To his critics who thought he was being soft, Neville stated, "We should seek by all means in our power to avoid war, by analyzing possible causes, by trying to remove them, by discussion in a spirit of collaboration and good will." Neville had another reason – a much more self-serving reason - for not angering Hitler as well. Although Neville was no fan of the Nazi Party, he believed that since the Nazi Party did not like the Communist Party, the Nazi Party was an ally in the effort to contain communism.

The German Nazi Party's relationship to the Russian Communist Party changed in August 1939. On that day Nazi

Germany and the U.S.S.R. became friends – at least on paper. In the last week of August 1939, the two nations signed a treaty claiming they would not attack each other; unknown to the rest of the world, they had also agreed how they would divide Poland.

On September 1, 1939, Germany invaded Poland from the west. The U.S.S.R. waited until the Polish troops were positioned to fight the Germans, and then it invaded from the East on September 16. Poland never officially surrendered to either power, but, by October 6, the two nations had completely secured Poland for themselves.

On September 3, the third day of the German invasion, Neville admitted to the English Parliament that his policies had failed. "This is a sad day for all of us, and to none is it sadder than to me. Everything that I have worked for, everything that I have hoped for, everything that I have believed in during my public life, has crashed into ruins." If you had been listening to the radio that day, you would have heard Neville say, "I am speaking to you from the Cabinet Room at 10 Downing Street. This morning the British Ambassador in Berlin handed the German Government an official note stating that unless we heard from them by eleven o'clock, that they were prepared at once to withdraw their troops from Poland, a state of war would exist between us. I have to tell you now that no such undertaking has been received, and consequently this country is at war with Germany."

The picture Hitler wanted for the world was not the picture that was in the United Kingdom's best interests, and Neville realized that the only way to stop the change was to fight against it. Neville led the war effort until a combination of British military setbacks and poor health forced him to resign as Prime Minister eight months into the war. The reluctant warrior whose name became a synonym for "appeasement" in his time was . . . **Neville Chamberlain.**

Moral
Change is coming.

CHAPTER 34

August 1945

Atomic Bombs Dropped on Japan

The Mice Who Made a Mouse Trap

Do you like to be notified ahead of time when things are likely to occur? I know I do. For instance, when the teacher tells us that there will be a test over the unit in three weeks, I mark the test on my calendar. Because I can see it coming, I can prepare for it and be ready for it. I may not be able to stop it from coming, but when it comes, I will be prepared.

In 1939, U.S. President Franklin Delano Roosevelt received a letter from Al. Al was employed as a science teacher in Germany, but he had been visiting the United States when Adolf Hitler had taken over Germany and he had not gone back. Al was still in touch with German scientists, and he had been made aware that Hitler's scientists knew how to split the atom. They still had a couple of issues to resolve to put the technology into the form of a bomb, but they were close to having the bomb. Al stated that Hitler would use the bomb as soon as he had it. Although he was born a German, Al made it clear that his loyalties lay with the Allies. Al did not want to see any country invent the atom bomb, but he believed the side that built the bomb first would win the war, and so he encouraged the President to pursue the bomb.

Al was a leading scientist in Germany, and the President believed everything Al wrote to be true. Just like you and I see a test in the future and prepare for it, the President now saw a German bomb in the future, and he prepared to build a bomb before the Germans did. He put together a group of scientists; the team called itself the Manhattan Project, but most of the work was actually done in Laos, New Mexico.

Despite the Germans working hard to build the technology, they did not get it built before the Allies began to make inroads into Germany. Berlin fell in 1945 before the bomb was completed.

The Manhattan Project was not sure, but in 1945 they thought they might have successfully built a bomb. They tested one in New Mexico, and it seemed to work. Although Germany was on the verge of surrender, Japan was not. To force Japan to surrender would likely take an invasion of the Japanese islands, and that was going to be very costly in both American lives and Japanese lives – but especially American lives. The Japanese had demonstrated their willingness to die for their country just to hurt America – kamikaze pilots would fly their planes deliberately into ships, knowing it would kill the pilot but also wipe out several Americans. Someone suggested dropping the bomb on Japan – it would be a way to test the technology and it might bring the war to a close.

Despite being the vice-president, Harry Truman was not aware of the top-secret Manhattan project. When President Roosevelt died in office, Harry Truman became the President. As President, it was his call whether to use the bomb against Japan. On August 26, the United States demanded that Japan surrender or face terrible destruction. When Japan did not surrender, President Truman authorized dropping the atom bomb code named "Little Boy" on Hiroshima, Japan on August 6, an area where no American prisoners of war were being held. When Japan still did not surrender, he authorized a second atom bomb, "Fat Man", to be dropped on a torpedo plant in Nagasaki, Japan. Japan surrendered at that time.

Al was glad the Allies had won, and he was especially glad that peace was restored. Al, though, knew that the bomb technology was now available and that other countries would soon have it too. He suspected that if any country were about to be annihilated in war, they would resort to using the bomb; although countries might say the atom bomb was there to keep other countries from attacking them for fear of mutual destruction, Al believed it was just a matter of time before someone used it - The world was drifting towards catastrophe.

Although he was not involved in the Manhattan project, he felt he was partly responsible for the technology of the bomb, and he stated he would never have become a scientist if this would have prevented the bomb from being created. "If only I had known, I would have become a watchmaker," he said earnestly. If he had been a watchmaker, we would not have the atom bomb, the Theory of Relativity, or know the name of . . . **Albert Einstein.**

Moral
Think ahead.

CHAPTER 35

OCTOBER 24, 1945
UNITED NATIONS FOUNDED

UNITED IN PEACE

Do you like group projects? I usually do. (The only time I do not is when someone dumps all the work on me.) Believe it or not, this book is a group project. My part is to write it. However, someone else came up with the idea for it, someone else will edit my work, someone else will draw the pictures, and someone else will make sure it gets to the printers. Without any of the team members, there would not be a book.

Teams are needed to make most things work. Having been through two world wars, nations were used to working with each other in times of war, Frank thought. The idea of working together in times of peace was a relatively new concept though. The League of Nations, formed after World War I, had not succeeded. Frank could see the nations were becoming more integrated, and he believed an international organization of all nations was needed. He was the first to use the term "United Nations." He ran his idea past his wartime peers - Winston Churchill, the Prime Minister of the United Kingdom, and Joseph Stalin, the Premier of the U.S.S.R.; they agreed the organization was needed.

From October 18 through November 1, 1943, delegates from the United States, United Kingdom, the U.S.S.R., and China met in Moscow to discuss the possibility of a United Nations. They released a document in which they stated that they "recognize[d] the necessity of establishing at the earliest practicable date a general international organization, based on the principle of the sovereign equality of all peace-loving States, and open to membership by all such States, large and small, for the maintenance of international peace and security." Then from November 28 – December 1, the three Allies – Roosevelt, Churchill, and Stalin – met in Tehran, Iran, declaring that they "shall work together in war and in the peace that will follow." They declared that they assumed "the supreme responsibility resting upon us and all the United Nations to make a peace which will command the goodwill of the overwhelming mass of the peoples of the world and banish the scourge and terror of war for many generations." The United Nations was not going to be a dictator, but rather a place where democracy ruled. They said they wanted to "seek the cooperation and active participation of all nations, large and small, whose peoples in heart and mind are dedicated, as are our own peoples, to the elimination of tyranny and slavery, oppression and intolerance" within a "world family of Democratic Nations."

On October 24, 1945, his vision became a reality – the United Nations Building in New York City opened its doors and allowed in delegates from throughout the world. Frank was not there – he had died suddenly, but the President of the United States, Harry Truman, delivered the opening remarks, saying, "We fully realize today that victory in war requires a mighty united effort. Certainly, victory in peace calls for, and must receive, an equal effort. Man has learned long ago that it is impossible to live unto himself. This same basic principle applies today to nations. We were not isolated during the war. We dare not now become isolated in peace."

If he had been alive, Frank would have delivered the opening remarks. In fact, when Frank unexpectedly died, people thought about postponing the opening. His successor, Harry Truman, believed in the organization just like he did, and Truman agreed to pick up any slack from Frank's untimely death. It made sense that Truman did that, for Truman was Frank's vice-president. That is right, the person who can be credited with founding the United Nations is U.S. President . . . Franklin Delano Roosevelt.

Moral
Cooperation is important.

CHAPTER 36

DECEMBER 10, 1948
UNITED NATIONS DECREES HUMAN RIGHTS

WHAT TO DO WHEN A DECREE IS NOT ENOUGH

Do you remember being born? Me neither. My earliest memory is from when I was three. I believe the doctors when they say everything is on video tape in our brain, but I do not know how to pull up any of the early tapes.

Were you born with certain rights? In reality, the answer is no. We are born with the rights that society assigns us. For instance, if I had been born of slave parents in the United States in 1820, I would have had no rights.

Being born a human being, though, should give people rights. All humans - regardless of which nation they are born, what their gender is, what color their skin is, how rich of a family they were born into, or how they have been wired mentally – should have these rights. If we believe in the Golden Rule of "do unto others as you would have them do unto you," then certain rights can be claimed at birth. One of the first issues the United Nations addressed was the question of human rights.

Eleanor Roosevelt, the widow of President Franklin Delano Roosevelt, was appointed by President Harry Truman as the first delegate from the United States to the United Nations in 1945. The United Nations then appointed her as chair of the United Nations Commission on Human Rights. As chair, she oversaw the creation of the Universal Declaration of Human Rights. The Universal Declaration of Human Rights declared that all people of all countries were born free and were of equal dignity. On December 10, 1948, 48 of the 58 countries that comprised the United Nations voted in favor of it; the rest abstained or were absent – no one voted against it.

Was this decree enforced? Nelson would be the first to tell you that it was not. Nelson was a civil rights activist in South Africa. In South Africa, the all-white government had declared that white people got special privileges and that skin tone determined one's rank in society. The system was known as apartheid. The United Nations opposed it verbally, but, aside from a boycott here and there, the United Nations did not take action to overthrow it.

Nelson, though, made it a point to overthrow apartheid. He began with civil disobedience, but, when that did not work, he encouraged people to become more militant. He also became more communist, having read much of Karl Marx's works. He was in and out of jail for his early acts of civil disobedience, but then spent 27 straight years in prison for his militant acts. He was out of sight but not forgotten; his wife Winnie made sure to keep his name in the news, and he became an icon for the removal of apartheid. In 1990, he was released and was perceived as a hero. The South African president who released him asked for his help to end apartheid and to set up elections for all races. Nelson agreed to help. Nelson actually won that 1994 election, and he became the leader of South Africa.

Nelson served one term as President, laying the framework for future rules by both his words and his deeds. If you ask any South African who the father of modern South Africa is, they will answer . . . **Nelson Mandela.**

Moral
Love everyone.

CHAPTER 37

1948
THE END OF COLONIZATION
TRUTH AND FIRMNESS

Have you ever noticed how much ground you cover in a single step? If you have a long stride, it might be a meter or two. A meter or two, though – that is not very much. However, when this is repeated many, many times, we move many kilometers. How do we move many kilometers? One meter at a time.

How do we usually bring about change? Is it sudden, or is it step by step? Most of the time, it is probably step by step. In fact, in many cases the steps are so insignificant that you may not even be aware of them. It is only when you look back that you can see how far you have come.

Mahatma – that is Indian for "great souled one" – realized that destinies were determined day by day, one step at a time. Mahatma was an Indian who was living in South Africa; his law practice in Bombay, India had not done well, and so he and his wife made a new start in South Africa. Both India and South Africa were part of the British Empire; they had lost their independence when the explorers had claimed the lands for the United Kingdom. In the early 1900s, nationalism was rising in both places.

Mahatma experienced discrimination in South Africa. He was asked to take off his turban; he was made to give up his seat for a European. Through nonviolent protests, he and his friends tried to end such discrimination. He referred to these actions as "truth and firmness," for he was going to tell the truth and stand firm in that truth even if the civil authorities did not like it.

In 1915, Mahatma went back to India. He supported the United Kingdom's war effort in World War I, but he sought independence for India. He organized both farmers and urban workers to stage civil disobedience with the goal of ending discrimination and reducing taxes. Mahatma believed that "peace is the most powerful weapon," and he believed India would get its independence if it resisted the temptation to go to war with the United Kingdom. In 1921, he became head of the Indian National Congress, and he began to put on nationwide strikes and other civil disobedience in the name of freedom of religion, women's rights, and rights for the poor. He himself wore an Indian loincloth to identify himself with the poor. In the winter, he added a locally made shawl to the loincloth; he stressed the local manufacturing aspect because he wanted India to become free of relying on British imports. Whereas some leaders lived in palaces and had lots of servants, Mahatma insisted on living in a humble dwelling and taking care of himself.

The cycle of civil disobedience, arrest, and release continued until 1947 when Mahatma's strategy of nonviolence succeeded; the British Empire granted India its freedom. However, instead of the one large religiously plural nation Mahatma envisioned, the United Kingdom made two nations: a Muslim Pakistan to the north and Hindu India to the south. Mahatma was selected to rule over the Hindu portion. He loved all people, and he worked closely with Muslims in his area who wanted to migrate to Pakistan. A lot of his citizens, though, were not as easy-going, and chaos often erupted. On January 12, 1948, a Hindu assassin fired three bullets into Mahatma at point-blank range.

Mahatma is considered the father of modern India. His birthday, October 2, is a national holiday in India. October 2 is also International Day of Nonviolence in his honor. Once the chaos from his assassination cleared, his daughter, Indira, emerged as leader of the Indian National Congress and became the leader of India; she carried on the legacy of her father . . . **Mohandas K. Gandhi.**

Moral
Do not be overwhelmed with big projects; take things one step at a time.

CHAPTER 38

MARCH 25, 1957
EUROPEAN ECONOMIC COMMUNITY FORMED

FROM MANY COMES ONE

Have you ever been to a carnival with a Midway; that is, a fair where they have a series of amusement rides and games you can play? I went to one last year, and we had to turn our U.S. dollars into Midway tickets. The Midway rides and games would not take U.S. dollars. The exchange rate varied at different times of the day; sometimes you could buy a lot more tickets with a dollar than you could at other times.

This was a problem that western Europe was having in 1945. Every country had its own currency, and to do business, you had to buy the other country's currency. There was a lot of destruction in Europe, and the raw material might be in one country, the factory in another, and a consumer in another, so the paperwork between countries became tedious.

Time was precious. The Soviet Union was able to churn out weapons and other goods quickly, and if western Europe could not keep up the pace, it risked being invaded and overrun by the Soviets, just as some eastern European countries had been. Winston, the leader who had served as Prime Minister of the United Kingdom during the war, had seen how the states of the United States cooperated. For instance, they had one currency, so people in one state could easily do business with people in another state. He liked what he saw in the United States, and he proposed that the European nations have a relationship like what the states had.

Winston had other reasons besides economic ones for wanting to see a united Europe. He believed that if Germany was a state of Europe, the other states could keep tabs on it. The radical military buildup that happened before World War II could be prevented. He also believed that if the western European countries worked as a block, they could stand up to the U.S.S.R.; otherwise, one by one they might fall into the U.S.S.R. orbit.

Winston passionately believed what he was saying, but he was no longer Prime Minister so he could not influence the United Kingdom as he had before. Many in the United Kingdom did not want to give up their freedom to a European power, and both those for and against a super-Europe realized that cooperating would mean not doing what they wanted to do from time to time.

The modern European Union was formed gradually. At first just a few nations participated, and then when others saw it working, they joined as well. Also, the European Union began with simple economic cooperation and waited until later to begin to undertake political issues. The European Economic Community was formed in 1957. The European Union as we know it was founded on Nov. 1, 1993, when participants signed the Maastricht Treaty.

The United Kingdom was a part of the European Union for a while – it voted to withdraw in 2016 and left in 2020. (As of this book being published, it is the only nation to have withdrawn from the European Union.) Would Winston have approved of it leaving? Who knows for sure? Although he came up with the idea and promoted the idea of a union, Winston had mixed feelings about the European Union as it was taking shape. The United Kingdom, though, definitely played a major role in laying the foundation, and the leader of that push was the United Kingdom's own former Prime Minister . . . **Winston Churchill.**

Moral
When we work with others, we cannot always have it entirely our way.

CHAPTER 39

OCTOBER 4, 1957
SPUTNIK LAUNCHED
THE SPACE RACE BEGINS

Have you ever noticed that everyone has someone who supervisors them? For instance, at school my teacher oversees me and my work. The principal oversees the teacher. The superintendent oversees the principal. The school board oversees the superintendent. The school board must answer to the voters, or the voters will not re-elect them.

Everybody has a boss. Even a one-person business must listen to their customers' requirements or else they will not remain in business. For instance, independent taxi drivers must do what their passenger's want. It should come as no surprise then that the people who built the first successful satellites had a boss.

Who this mastermind was behind the U.S.S.R. satellites and the Mir space station, though, was a state secret until 1987; he worked in obscurity for over thirty years! The U.S.S.R. citizens would hear him congratulating the Russian cosmonauts – we would call them astronauts – on television, but they could not see his face. He stunned the world again and again with his accomplishments. His first accomplishment was the launching of the world's first satellite. On October 4, 1957, he launched Sputnik – "Sputnik" is a Russian for "world traveler," a 183.9-pound satellite that was the size of a beach ball; the satellite orbited the earth in 98 minutes. Most people in the United States and western Europe had believed that the West was way ahead of the U.S.S.R. technologically, but now realized they were not. Russia's advanced knowledge sent trembles of fear across the United States and western Europe. The launch was a wake-up call. The United States became serious about space science.

It even evaluated its school curriculum, realizing it needed to stress much more math and science.

The unknown mastermind followed up Sputnik with Sputnik II on November 2, 1957; Sputnik II was the first time that a mammal – the dog Laika – was ever in space. In 1961, he put the first human being into space.

Meanwhile, the space exploration program in the United States was not going well. The United States tried to launch its first satellite on December 6, 1957, but it exploded on the launch pad. On February 5 and on March 5 of 1958, it had two more satellites that failed to launch. United States Senator and soon-to-be-President John F. Kennedy summed up the nation's frustration, saying, "The first man-made satellite to orbit the earth was named Sputnik. The first living creature in space was Laika. The first rocket to the Moon carried a red flag. The first photograph of the far side of the Moon was made with a Soviet camera. If a man orbits the earth this year his name will be Ivan." Kennedy believed the West had to enter space before or at least with the Russians; otherwise, space would be purely U.S.S.R. territory. Finally, on March 17,1958 the United States showed signs of being able to challenge the U.S.S.R.; it successfully launched Vanguard One, its first successful satellite.

The secret general, the rocket mastermind, was unknown to even most Russians until 1987, when he was mentioned by name in the Pravda newspaper in 1987. Despite his identity being out as of 1987, he continued working through to 1991, and was the architect behind the Mir Space Station. After retiring, he wrote a book of the history of the Soviet space program, *The Way to Space*. The Soviet Azerbaijani genius who changed the world was . . . **Kerim Kerimov.**

Moral
Do the job right, and any glory due will likely eventually find you.

CHAPTER 40

JULY 10, 1962
TELSTAR SATELLITE LAUNCHED
THE MOST TRUSTED MAN IN AMERICA

My dad was there and saw it firsthand – even though he really was not there. He had a firsthand view of the men walking on the moon in 1969; he saw people scrambling to get pieces of the Berlin Wall for a souvenir; and he watched as the first bombs dropped on Iraq during the Gulf War. He saw all these firsthand – from his living room chair.

Prior to 1962, none of this would have been possible. Although he might have heard radio reports, he could not have seen it live as it was happening. (He could have seen it live on pre-recorded tape but not live in real time.) In 1962, though, the world became a much smaller place, and a person in the United States could see first-hand what other people were doing just by turning on the news on one's television set.

On July 10, 1962, the United States launched Telstar, a satellite that could broadcast pictures across the Atlantic Ocean. It was like looking out one's front window; the event may have been happening thousands of miles away, but one could see the details as if one were right there with the participants.

The Columbia Broadcast System (CBS) recognized this new technology and created a daily video magazine for people, the CBS Evening News. The show began in 1962, almost immediately when the technology was in place. They selected Walter to be the news anchor, the person who explained what the film clip was about.

Walter was one of the most trusted people in the United States; when he said something, most people accepted it as the truth. He had been a broadcast reporter since 1937, and he had covered World War II, the Nuremberg trials in which suspected Nazi leaders were tried, and the Vietnam War. Walter accepted the job; he became a nightly fixture in numerous American homes from 1962 until he retired in 1981. Numerous Americans learned about the happenings of the world through Walter.

Walter believed in a free press, and he shared the news "as it is," trying not to let any personal bias or political preference slip into it. Many in the U.S. government were not happy with Walter's program. When Americans were treated to pictures of soldiers dying in Vietnam, many lost the appetite for war. Walter was just showing the way it was, but many in the government considered him a liberal. Walter did not care what labels people gave him – "If that is what makes us liberals, so be it, just as long as in reporting the news we adhere to the first ideals of good journalism - that news reports must be fair, accurate and unbiased;" he just wanted to educate Americans.

Walter did not think that most people were as informed about current events as they should be. He believed this resulted in people making poorly informed decisions at the voting polls – "We are not educated well enough to perform the necessary act of intelligently selecting our leaders." Walter was especially concerned about American illiteracy – "We've got a great percentage of our population that, to our great shame, either cannot or, equally unfortunate, will not read. And that portion of our public is growing. Those people are suckers for the demagogue" – and worried that these people could be easily conned by shrew advertisers and politicians.

Each night Walter would end his newscast saying, "And that's the way it is." People could now see events happening throughout the world, and people like Walter were there to explain what and why they were seeing it. The world was becoming much more tight-knit, and what happened in one part of the world could have immediate ripples in another part of the world. The Telstar Satellite changed the world, and the way Walter shared the information became the norm of how such information should be shared not just in the United States but around the world. Next time you see a "talking head" on the news and a camera going live, think of where it all began – with Telstar Satellite and . . . **Walter Cronkite.**

Moral
Report the facts without bias.

CHAPTER 41

July 21, 1969

Moon
Walk

To the Moon and Back

Do you have a nickname? If so, what does it refer to? Do you know who first gave it to you?

Nicknames are usually a term of endearment. (Notice the word "usually." When a bully gives you a nickname, it is usually not a nice nickname, and it certainly is not a term of endearment.) Nicknames are usually assigned based on a physical trait or an interest. For instance, "Stretch" may be a tall person; "Shorty" may be a short person; and "Blondie" may be a girl with blonde hair. Sometimes the nickname is the deliberate opposite of the characteristic. For instance, the tallest person in our class is called "Tiny." Nicknames that suggest interests include things like calling the boy who enjoys attending church "Reverend" or calling the girl who loves drumming "Sticks." Sometimes, too, a nickname is given because it rhymes with their real name. For instance, "Downtown" Larry Brown and "Bad" Brad. "Bad" Brad may be one of the nicest people you will ever meet, but because "bad" rhymes with "Brad", the name sticks. Always check to see if the person likes the nickname before you call them by it; you do not want to hurt any feelings.

Edwin had a nickname, "Buzz." He earned it at an early age, and it followed him through his life. It began because his sister could not pronounce the word "Brother", so when she called to him, she would say "Buzzer." His whole family started to call him "Buzzer," which eventually evolved into "Buzz." His astronaut peers and others tried to give him other nicknames, but none stuck.

Buzz was an astronaut. Buzz had already made three spacewalks in his career as part of the Gemini Eleven mission. That was in 1966. Now, three years later, on July 21, 1969, he was on the most dangerous mission of his career. As a fighter pilot for the United States Air Force, he had flown 66 missions in the Korean War and had shot down two MIG-15s; he was used to flying and used to danger – he had nerves of steel. On this day, he was to take flight commander Neil Armstrong from the Apollo 11 spacecraft in a lunar module and land the craft on the moon.

They left Michael Collins to monitor Apollo 11 and began their descent to the moon. Things did not go as planned. The lunar module was going faster than intended, and the astronauts overshot the desired landing spot. As they looked for a spot to land, they began to run low on fuel. To complicate things more, emergency sirens began to blow and flashed Code 1212; despite all their training neither Neil Armstrong nor Buzz knew what that meant. Mission Control radioed to ignore it; it was later explained that Buzz had the radar on, and the computer was having trouble keeping up with the calculations. The moon's surface was rocky, but, with only about 45 seconds worth of fuel left, Buzz had to land; he gently lowered the module, resulting in three of the four lunar-probes legs touching the moon's rocky surface. After completing the checklist, mission control stated, "We copy you down, Eagle." Neil Armstrong confirmed, letting Mission Control and the world know, "The Eagle has landed."

Buzz depressurized the cabin and the hatch to exit was opened. NASA had predetermined Neil would go out first and had built the exit hatch on his side – they justified this decision because he was both the commander, and he was known for humility. As Neil stepped from the lunar module to the moon's surface, he told Buzz and the world, "I'm going to step off the LM [lunar module] now. That's one small step for [a] man and one giant leap for mankind." Buzz joined his friend walking on the moon's surface 19 minutes later.

When the 1960s had begun, U.S. President John F. Kennedy had told the U.S. Congress, "We choose to go to the moon in this decade and do the other things, not because they are easy, but because they are hard, because that goal will serve to organize and measure the best of our energies and skills, because that challenge is one that we are willing to accept, one we are unwilling to postpone, and one which we intend to win." In July 1969, at the end of the decade, two American astronauts stood on the moon's surface – **Neil Armstrong and Edwin "Buzz" Aldrin.**

Moral
Give yourself challenging goals.

CHAPTER 42

APRIL 22, 1970
EARTH DAY/WORLD-WIDE
CELEBRATING THE EARTH

Earth Day occurs April 22 of each year. What do you do to celebrate Earth Day? At my school last year, we collected cans and newspapers for recycling. We also planted a tree on the school lawn.

The first Earth Day occurred in 1970. Its founder, a United States Senator named Gaylord, wanted to promote awareness of how great the Earth was and to help people appreciate the natural environment. The first Earth Day was targeted to U.S. children, as the future of their country. Gaylord wrote to all the U.S. colleges and placed an article in the popular kids' magazine Scholastic to tell everyone about it and to suggest ways to celebrate it.

Stewardship of the Earth affects everyone, and soon other countries started celebrating Earth Day too. By 1990, 140 countries were celebrating it, and by 2012, that number had climbed to 175. Today Earth Day is the most celebrated environmental event in the world.

Earth Day causes people to focus on the Earth for at least one day. Because of this focus, people have taken time to become aware of some people-created problems with the earth – acid rain, litter, polluted streams, deadly pesticides, and climate change - and have been forced to face them. The 1970 Earth Day is credited with directly inspiring the Environmental Protection Agency in the United States and with stimulating thinking that resulted in the Clean Air Act, the Clean Water Act, and the Endangered Species Act.

Earth Day events are planned at the local level; no country has a government agency dictating what to do. You and your classmates can determine the best way to celebrate in your community. Suggestions are to clean up a vacant lot, to pick up litter, to plant a tree, and to make educational posters to hang in nearby stores. YOU can make a difference.

Having people in nations around the world becoming conscious of the Earth and trying to be good stewards of it is a major, major change in the psychology of almost all generations past when people did not know or did not care about being good stewards. In fact, most generations had seen humans at war with the environment, trying to subdue it. In the 1990s, Vice President Al Gore of the United States called knowledge about people's harmful effects on the environment "An Inconvenient Truth" because most people did not want to change. People did change, though, and are continuing to change, thanks to Earth Day, which was created by . . . **Gaylord Nelson.**

Moral
Be a good steward of the Earth.

CHAPTER 43

1973
DIGITAL REVOLUTION
RISE OF THE INTERNET

Have you ever heard the expression that necessity is the mother of invention? This means that if we see a need, then we try to find a way to fill that need. If we are not aware of the need or if life is going great, then we will not create the invention.

In the 1960s, the United States military realized that it had a problem. The military had begun to store data on computers, and it realized that if the U.S.S.R was able to destroy the super-computer with all the nation's data, the United States would be practically helpless. Leaders decided that, rather than try to protect one super-computer, the United States should create a network of computers that interacted with one another, but should one of the computers be destroyed, the rest would keep running and no information lost. As my grandmother would say, it was a strategy built around "don't put all of your eggs in one basket."

Having an idea is one thing, being able to turn that idea into reality is something else. Bob was up to the challenge, though. Bob was an employee of the U.S. Information Processing Transmission Office (IPTO). He was aware of existing network protocols and built the Transmission Control Protocol (TCP). TCP allowed computers to speak to each other, regardless of what the hardware was, what software they were running, or where in the world they were located.

Vint Cerf joined Bob in the lab. They decided to use TCP for host-to-host communication and Internet Protocol (IP) for internetwork communication. The final product was a code - TCP/IP (Transmission Control Protocol/Internet Protocol), a suite of communication protocols used to interconnect network devices on the Internet. This is the figurative handshake that links two computers together.

Today, any computer can be used to send information, to broadcast news and music, to work on joint business projects, and to play games against each other. Using Internet cables and Bluetooth, your computer can communicate with computers around the world – as well as with the person next door.

Bob eventually became director of IPTO. He continued to work with Vint, and in 1972 they founded the Internet Society, an organization to provide education, standards, and policy about the Internet. If you use the Internet, you are using a product that was built by . . . **Bob Kahn.**

Moral
Make the Internet work for you.

CHAPTER 44

1980
YOKO SHIMOMURA

MARIO, LUIGI, AND PRINCESS PEACH OWE THEIR SUCCESS TO HER

Have you ever played a video game?

In the late 1970s, video games became a household phenomenon for much of the world. To say that one person invented the video game is silly; numerous people had various firsts in the field. Although the field was – and is - considered a man's field, numerous women have contributed to it as well. For instance, a schoolteacher, Mabel Addis, designed the first text-based strategy game, The Sumerian Game, in 1964. Video games were very popular in the early 1980s, but so many poor-quality games were made that by the mid-1980s people no longer respected the products of the gaming industry.

People such as Yoko, though, did not sacrifice quality in the attempt to make a fast buck. She and her coworkers poured their hearts into Street Fighter II: The World Warrior, all of the Kingdom Hearts games, Parasite Eve, Final Fight, Mario and Luigi: Superstar Saga, and Final Fantasy XV; and the games became hits, reviving an industry. Having rescued the industry, Yoko continued to work in it, most recently on Super Smash Bros. Ultimate and Xenoblade Chronicles: Definitive Edition.

Just as it is a myth that only men are in the video game field, it is a myth that all people in the field are computer nerds. Unlike most people in the video game field, Yoko wasn't a programmer – York was a musician. She had played video games in her youth but had never pictured herself making them. She had studied to be a piano instructor, but, when she had the invitation to go into unchartered territory as a female composer for video games, she shocked her family and took it. Yoko resisted the temptation to turn out cheap, easy music, and instead presented quality scores that truly enhanced the games. She took the industry's music from a mere background theme to a true musical score; she said she wanted to make music that was enticing and yet thought-provoking. Her scores are so complex that they have been translated into piano scores and have even been placed on albums. If you have ever played any of the games listed above, you have likely heard an original composition by . . . **Yoko Shimomura.**

Moral
Quality matters.

CHAPTER 45

2012
MALALA YOUSAFZAI
DO YOU WANT TO GO TO SCHOOL TODAY?

Now, be honest, do you want to go to school today?

If you are like my friends, the answer is no. They would much rather sit at home playing video games or run around the neighborhood having adventures.

Going to school is a privilege we have in the United States – in fact, it is the law that you must attend school until you are at least sixteen years-old, so we take going to school for granted. We believe it will always be there and we welcome breaks from it.

In some parts of the world, though, this is not the case. School is not something that children have a natural right to, especially if they are girls. For these people, going to school is rare, and most would gladly answer yes to the question of wanting to go to school.

Malala, a Pakistani girl, is an example of a student who wanted to go to school but was told that she could not by many in her society. In fact, on October 9, 2012, a member of the Taliban found her while she was riding a bus, put a gun to her head, and shot her as an example to other girls who might seek education.

The terrorist's goal of making Malala an example worked, but not with the results he wanted. When Malala had recovered from the gunshot wound, she willingly risked her life and went back to school. When the other boys and girls saw the effort that she made to come to school, they realized just how important getting an education was. They realized that education would enhance their knowledge, creativity, and problem-solving skills. They also realized that education would make them independent of others, such as the Taliban that wanted to keep them dumb and ignorant. For her efforts, Malala won a Nobel Peace Prize in 2014; at the age of seventeen, she was the youngest to ever win the prize. Through her writings and her deeds, she has continued to promote both women's rights and education.

Sometimes we think of historical figures as people of the past, but people in the present are changing history too. Sometimes we think that we are the wrong skin color, too young or too old, too rural, or too urban, and/or not the right gender to make a difference, but most people who change history are everyday people like us who rise to an occasion, such as . . . **Malala Yousafzai.**

Moral
Don't take your rights for granted.

CHAPTER 46

2011 - 2020
MARS EXPLORATION
DREAM IT AND DO IT

Do you like to fail? I do not. It stings and it is embarrassing.

However, I fail all the time. You are reading an article I got published; I am embarrassed to tell you how many have been rejected. On Friday nights you may see me at the roller rink doing some fancy skating moves, but have you ever stopped to realize how many times I must have fallen to get that good?

The truth is, if you are not failing, you are not pushing yourself. To grow, we must try new things, and when we try new things, we often fail. You must be comfortable failing. You should not be satisfied with failure, but you must realize that to become good at something you are going to fail many times along the way.

Elon, an American inventor, has great visions for the world. He can picture rockets carrying private citizens to the moon. In 2002 he began SpaceX, and he now has the technology to dock a person on the International Space Station. Going to Mars and beyond are possibilities, and he envisions a human colony on Mars with over one million people. He also envisions pleasure trips there, saying, "Land on Mars; a round ticket – half a million dollars. It can be done."

Elon also pictures the world without gas cars. He became the chair of the board and product architect at Tesla in 2008. Although he was not involved when the company began in 2008, he is considered a co-founder because of the huge imprint he has had on the organization. In addition to creating more efficient models, he has expanded from electric cars into electric pickups. Not only has he tried to improve the efficiency of the design of the car, but he has tried to create a better battery as well.

Elon has already had a lot of success. He developed a secure, fast method for managing money on the Internet; he started X.com, which became PayPal. He has been phenomenally successful in the past with social-media Internet technology too; he created YouTube and LinkedIn.

Elon dabbles in a wide variety of fields. He created the Boring Company – not the "it's a drag" but a "let us dig a tunnel" tunnel company. He plans to make an underground walkway around the Las Vegas Convention Center. He was an advisor to U.S. President Donald Trump. He has become one of the wealthiest people in the world even though he claims, "For me it was never about money but solving problems for the future of humanity." Elon is a problem solver, an inventor, and an entrepreneur. He can foresee a world where space travel is routine and where electric cars are the norm, and he is seeking to bring that vision to reality.

Many people have laughed at Elon when he has shared his dreams, but Teslas are on the road today and Space X is docking at the International Space Station – his far-fetched visions just might come to pass. He still says some strange things- and some of his "science" is questionable to many; he may be proven right in the future. Still, Elon's genius cannot be denied, and his inventions are changing the way many people go about life. Unlike many of the people in this book, Elon has already transformed banking, social media, and transportation, and he is still relatively young. Expect to hear a lot more about . . . **Elon Musk.**

Moral
Dream big – and then strive to make your dreams come true.

Did you enjoy the book?

If you did, we are ecstatic. If not, please write your complaint to us and we will ensure we fix it.

If you're feeling generous, there is something important that you can help me with – tell other people that you enjoyed the book.

Ask a grown-up to write about it on Amazon. When they do, more people will find out about the book. It also lets Amazon know that we are making kids around the world laugh. Even a few words and ratings would go a long way.

If you have any ideas or jokes that you think are super funny, please let us know. We would love to hear from you. Our email address is -

riddleland@riddlelandforkids.com

Other Fun Books By Riddleland
Riddles Series

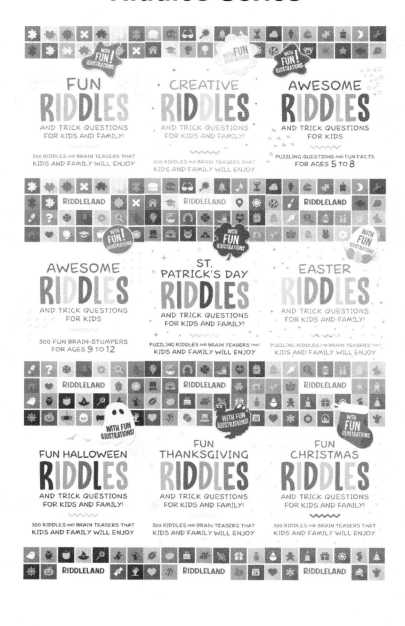

Its Laugh O'Clock Joke Books

It's Laugh O'Clock Would You Rather Books

**Get them on Amazon
or our website at www.riddlelandforkids.com**

About Riddleland

Riddleland is a mum + dad run publishing company. We are passionate about creating fun and innovative books to help children develop their reading skills and fall in love with reading. If you have suggestions for us or want to work with us, shoot us an email at

riddleland@riddlelandforkids.com

Our family's favorite quote:

"Creativity is an area in which younger people
have a tremendous advantage since
they have an endearing habit of always
questioning past wisdom and authority."
~ Bill Hewlett

Made in the USA
Las Vegas, NV
06 August 2023

75723997R00079